TO
SEE THE FACE OF
GOD

TO
SEE THE FACE OF
GOD

*Daily Meditations For The
Advent Season*

*

Rev. John P. Henry

ALBA · HOUSE   NEW · YORK

SOCIETY OF ST. PAUL, 2187 VICTORY BLVD., STATEN ISLAND, NEW YORK 10314

242.33

Library of Congress Cataloging-in-Publication Data

Henry, John P.
    To see the face of God / John P. Henry
      p.   cm.
    ISBN 0-8189-0569-7
    1. Advent — Meditations.   I. Title.
    BX2170.A4H46   1989   89-27164
    242'.33 — dc20   CIP

Designed, printed and bound in the United States of
America by the Fathers and Brothers of the
Society of St. Paul, 2187 Victory Boulevard,
Staten Island, New York 10314, as part of their
communications apostolate.

Printing Information:

Current Printing - first digit 1 2 3 4 5 6 7 8 9 10 11 12

Year of Current Printing - first year shown

1989   1990   1991   1992   1993   1994   1995   1996

DEDICATED

to the memory of
my parents

MARGARET AND JOHN

who taught me how to wait
for the one who is coming

ACKNOWLEDGMENT

Scripture texts used in this work are taken from
The New American Bible
copyright 1970
by the Confraternity of Christian Doctrine,
Washington, D.C.

TABLE OF CONTENTS

INTRODUCTION

Religion is boring! Christianity is boring! God is boring! In response to such complaints we reply that there's nothing boring about angels flying through a night sky ringing with a vibrant chorus praising God. There's nothing boring about shepherds having visions. Certainly there's nothing boring about virgins having babies. It's guaranteed that anyone who shares in the wonder of Christmas, the unimaginable, extraordinary reality of God becoming flesh, will never be bored again.

Advent is a time of waiting. There's expectancy in the air. It's essential that we know what we're expecting to happen, what we're waiting for, because otherwise when the weeks of Advent conclude, when Christmas dawns, we'll be confused, left alone and still waiting on a dark and empty morning. Our future literally hangs in the balance, dependent on recognizing and welcoming him when he comes.

Advent is a time of preparing. Unless we make effective use of the days of Advent to prepare for the one who's coming, our Christmas world will be one of sleigh bells and candy canes, snow flakes and punch bowls, mood music and dreamy religious tableaus, the termination of a cleverly designed merchandising scheme dramatically staged with a countdown of the shopping days remaining until Christmas.

Advent is a time of anticipation revealing the gradually unfolding plan of God's love and desire for us. That love, plan and desire are not distant, remote or impersonal. Jesus came to touch more than the contemporaries of his day. By our response to the graces of this season of waiting and preparing not only will we celebrate the wonder of the birth of our Savior on Christmas Day, but we will share in the reality of his coming to us personally in spirit, in power and in life now at this moment of our existence, as well as to be prepared to wait in expectant awe for his return at the end of time as he has promised. Advent begins our exploration of the mystery of God who was made flesh, renews our remembering of God's eternal love, prepares us to experience that love at this moment in time and brings us to anticipate his final coming to lead us home with him when created time has run its course. Advent gives a vision of his three comings — in the past, in the present and in the future. Each coming is real, each one an integral part of our Advent preparation and our Christmas celebration.

Advent is not a place for blinded groping, a season for vague hopes. It is a time to take firm hold of the hand of God in scripture and walk with him during the weeks of preparing for the Christmas event, a time to listen closely as he speaks to us in the daily liturgical readings of the Advent season. There we will find the gradual unfolding revelation of the credentials of the one who is coming. The Advent scriptures will focus our attention on promises made, preparing us for the extraordinary fulfillment of those promises. Speaking to us God himself will guide us to the triple Christmas celebration.

Time must be carved out of each Advent day to ensure a well founded, developing personal preparation for Christ's coming to us. Since the scripture readings are the presence of God to us in time, they are at the heart of our preparation. It is suggested that the process each day should be simple: read the scripture texts for the day, read the commentary for the appropriate day found in this book, re-read the texts, and then conclude the study with a fifteen minute meditation or contemplation. Scripture study and reflection should always lead to prayer, to immersion in the reality of the living God.

This is a book about waiting, about promises, about desire, about hope, about fulfillment. It is designed to help the waiting which will lead us to an event which is neither too shocking nor too ridiculous. May the season of Advent prepare us to celebrate a love and an embrace which defies created restrictions. May it prepare us to see the face of God.

*Daily Meditations For The
Advent Season*

Jesus Comes Bringing Us Peace and Healing

"Our Savior is coming. Have no more fear." That announcement in the entrance antiphon of today's Eucharistic liturgy stirs our hearts as the curtain rises on the Advent stage. The message proclaiming this Advent theme pours hope into listless spirits.

Too much space and so much time in life is consumed by fears and worries about our past personal history, our present tenuous relationship with our God and most especially with questions concerning our response to God in the unknown future. But today we are invited by our approaching Savior to surrender any anxieties we have regarding the Divine punishment or condemnation we feel is justly deserved as a result of our history of sinful rebellion. Such fears are a demonstration of an absence of hope, a lack of trust in God's mercy and forgiveness. At the same time we are moved to abandon any insecurity we feel about our future faithfulness to God because of our own human weakness and limitations.

"Lord I am not worthy," we protest with the centurion of today's gospel. Yet, like that centurion who recognized his need for Jesus to cure his sick servant, so also we know our profound need for Jesus to come and cure us. As the Lord responded so generously to the centurion's pleas, so also he desires to come to us, whatever our need, wherever he can find us. "I will come and cure him," is the unimaginable promise each of us must hear as our Advent days begin.

Today at the dawn of Advent we are reassured that, as the Lord once came to bring peace, strength and healing to a weak and broken world, he now comes to each one of us personally this Advent and Christmas. Only now is our redemption taking place; only now at this point in time are we individually, personally challenged to accept or reject Jesus as our Lord and Savior. Our personal preparation for welcoming the Lord as an integral participant in our existence begins by stirring up weak and broken spirits, spirits paralyzed by fear, to accept the reality of peace and the experience of healing which the Lord reaches out to offer us by his personal touch in our lives.

Jesus will give us peace when he comes. Isaiah assures us of that gift from the Lord in today's first scripture reading. Reflecting on this word of God we can already hear the distant echo of angels' voices clearly echoing in Bethlehem's night sky announcing the arrival of the Prince of Peace: "Glory to God . . . and peace on earth!" The peace Jesus brings is not the sort of peace which follows the termination of hostilities which is negotiated by means of a truce agreement. Nor is it the peace we sometimes experience in profound personal psychological calm. Neither is it the kind of unnatural, temporary peace sometimes fabricated by an escape from the human experience which is the normal lot of humanity this side of eternity.

The peace which the Lord brings to those who accept him can best be compared to the peace experienced by family members sharing a meal together. Fullness and satisfaction normally occurs when food is consumed, but a family meal involves much more than eating food. Most especially around that family table in the course of time a mutual acceptance of one another begins to be solidly fashioned. As a result of that acceptance no more is ever asked of anyone there than what each one is capable of giving. No one is asked to be any more than they actually are. The family meal never becomes the place for confrontation, unforgiveness, hostility, malice, uncharitableness or revenge. It is ever the place and the occasion for unity, love and peace among those gathered there to share a meal together. The peace of a family meal is a remedy for neglect, alienation and indifference. With an appreciation of that setting it is easy to see why Jesus chose the image of a banquet to portray the reality of heaven's joy, of eternal peace.

Welcoming the Prince of Peace will bring humanity to fulfill today's prophecy of Isaiah: "They shall beat their swords into plowshares and their spears into pruning hooks." The action of peace portrayed in that dramatic image should be the firm foundation for our participation in the Greeting of Peace which we offer at Mass to our brothers and sisters in Christ immediately before sharing the Eucharistic Meal with them. Today's theme of peace should leave us with a nagging question: "Can we ever share the eternal banquet of heaven with each other unless our relationship with one another here on earth is firmly founded on the peace brought to us by the Prince of Peace?"

Jesus comes bringing us healing as well as peace. He told the centurion in today's gospel: "I will come and cure . . .", and the miracle he performed then brought peace to the paralyzed body of the centurion's servant. Aware of our need for being made whole, of being cured, our paralyzed and broken spirits are roused by the urgent announcement of the entrance antiphon: "Our Savior is coming. Have no more fear." We have to be healed from our paralysis to become fit so that we will be able to respond to the invitation in today's first scripture reading: "Come . . . climb the Lord's mountain . . . that he may instruct us in his ways and we may walk in his paths."

The centurion of today's gospel is our model of faith. He trusted Jesus and as a result his servant was healed. We need the same kind of trust that God will heal us. Cured of our paralysis we can join those described by Isaiah today as streaming towards the Lord's house, as well as those pictured by Jesus in the gospel as coming from the east and west to claim their place at the family banquet table of God. Our Savior is coming to heal us, to cure us, to bring us peace, to lead us to the banquet table of God's family.

Today's Scripture Readings:

> *Isaiah 2:1-5;   Psalm 122:1-9;*
> *Matthew 8:5-11.*

Today's Advent Prayer:

> *"Our savior is coming. Have no more fear."*

TUESDAY — FIRST WEEK OF ADVENT

Jesus Comes Bringing
New Vision

Echoes of yesterday's entrance song to Advent fill the air as this new Advent day dawns: "Our Savior is coming. Have no more fear." But we do fear, especially when we cannot see. Many of us have had the frightening experience of being marooned in a room that suddenly became as dark as a blackened night because of power failure. We became bewildered, uncertain and fearful, losing our sense of direction and the location of things in a place where we always felt everything was very familiar. It is then that we experience the fearful handicap of living with blindness.

Our Savior is coming to us now that we might see. "See, the Lord is coming. . . . Then there will be endless day." Like a trumpet blast today's brief entrance antiphon lifts our faltering hearts, raises our downcast eyes to prepare us to welcome the one who is coming, the one who will introduce himself as "the light of the world." When he comes there will be darkness no longer. "Then there will be endless day." The night will be over. That is precisely what Jesus explains in the gospel reading: "Blessed are the eyes that see what you see."

The lyrics of a royal psalm composed without doubt for a king's coronation dominate this day of Advent. The new king is of royal lineage. He is not a usurper. That king is the one for whom we wait. He is a shoot from David, king of the Jewish nation. The one who is coming to us now is of that royal family. "And so Joseph went from the town of Nazareth in Galilee to David's town of Bethlehem — because he was of the house and lineage of David — to register with Mary, his espoused wife, who was with child. While they were there . . . she gave birth to her firstborn son." The dynasty of David suddenly continues, springs to life once again. The dry stump and dormant roots of Jesse are revived in the king who is coming, a person characterized in these words of Isaiah in the first scripture reading today: "The spirit of the Lord shall rest upon him."

As the prophet continues his description of this ideal king from David's line he portrays a fascinating paradise he will create where all creatures will live in peace, trust and harmony. Wolves and lambs, leopards and goats, calves and lions, cows and bears, lions and cattle, babies and poisonous snakes will compatibly live together without fear of annihilation. That sounds like a great fantasy, like a fairy tale, an impossible dream, a grand illusion. To live with such expectation is to act like a child. Yet the Lord, speaking gospel truth, invites us to childlike behavior, reminding us: "Father . . . what you have hidden from the learned and the clever you have revealed to the merest children."

Isaiah announces a message of hope to a world corrupted by sin and evil, to a humanity blinded by passion and selfishness. The prophet speaks of peace, justice and reconciliation to creatures who have concluded that their rebellious actions can only result in the horrors of justified punishment. Hopelessly blinded eyes are momentarily given the vision of a kingdom to be created in a Messianic age which is about to begin, announced by a king about to come on the human scene, to be finally fulfilled and completed when Christ the King comes again at the end of the ages.

Christmas is for children — children know how to enjoy a celebration. Advent is for children — children know how to bubble with anxious expectation when some wonderful thing is about to happen. In addition, a child knows how to trust, how to live with faith in someone, how to be hopeful, how to depend on someone else's care of them. The mystery of their father's love and his desire for their happiness is enthusiastically accepted without question or doubt by a child. In today's gospel Jesus tells us that we have to become like children if we are ever going to be able to grasp the extent of God our Father's love for us and the unimaginable reality of God becoming flesh. "Father . . . what you have hidden from the learned and the clever you have revealed to the merest children."

Today we ask the Lord to focus our eyes not only that we might recognize the one who is coming as the fulfillment of God's promises to us, but also that we might personally accept the wonder of a Father's love that he will reveal to us.

Today's Scripture Readings:

> *Isaiah 11:1-10; Psalm 72:1, 7-8, 12-13, 17;*
> *Luke 10:21-24.*

Today's Advent Prayer:

> *"Blest are the eyes that see what you see."*

WEDNESDAY — FIRST WEEK OF ADVENT

Jesus, The Good Shepherd, Comes To Heal and Feed

The people in today's gospel go to the mountain where they discover the power of God demonstrated by Jesus. Once again God reveals his presence on the heights just as he manifested himself on Mount Sinai and the Mount of Transfiguration.

As we join the people on the mountain crowding around Jesus we are jolted by the deafening roar of shouts and cries hurled in his direction by those demanding his attention. We find ourselves caught in the surging wave of humanity pressing and pushing toward him. Cries for help, some weak and plaintive, others demanding and desperate, screams coming from every segment of the mob as men and women, many with newly found energy hauled from the depths of weakened bodies, try to push themselves or carry others close to Jesus. He is their last hope. In sickness and pain some are already half dead. The disabled and the handicapped know the experience of rejection by society, have lived on the fringes of decent human existence, most often treated as non-entities, valued as worthless, as good as dead. Pleas are answered as "the cripples, the blind, the deaf and many others besides" are miraculously cured. Their living death has been destroyed. Jesus has triumped over death. We listen to the cries of astonishment, joy and

gratitude of those cured which are mingled with the frantic
calls of others seeking their miracle. Isaiah's prophecy in
today's reading has been fulfilled:

> "On this mountain the Lord of hosts
> > will provide for all people . . .
> The Lord God will wipe away the tears
> > from all faces . . .
> On that day it will be said:
> > 'Behold our God, to whom we look to save us!
> This is the Lord for whom we looked;
> > let us rejoice and be glad that he has saved us!'
> For the hand of the Lord will rest on this mountain."

Cripples now dance, the mute now sing, the blind now
see. There is a rising chorus of glory — wonder, gratitude
and praise — soon rising from that mountain. We're present
at the scene. We never want to leave there, to separate
ourselves from Jesus who still sits dominating the spectacle.
He has fulfilled Isaiah's prophecy that death would be destroyed and that tears would be wiped from all faces. People
have been cured. Now almost immediately he will bring
broadening smiles to more than four thousand faces who
are made his guests in the miracle of a meal he is about to
provide. "On this mountain the Lord . . . will provide . . . a
feast."

In time Jesus will describe himself as the Good
Shepherd; he will assume the Messianic title. Now, as we
recall the prayerful psalm: "The Lord is my shepherd," here
on this mountain he has cured the sick and injured of his
flock. Soon "moved with pity," he spreads a meal before
them.

Food is a preoccupation of a majority of people on earth today. In their hunger food is too often an obsession, their sole concern. We Americans for the most part are spoiled by the food available to us. Our concern is deciding what we shall eat, while many people in the world, even in our own country, are anxious about whether they will have anything to eat at all. The latter concern in that scenario is the reality to be grasped in the context of today's gospel meal. For most people in the world of Jesus' time and in our world today to have hunger satisfied is, simply stated, to have had a feast.

In the gospel description of this event it should not escape our eyes that "giving thanks he broke . . . and gave," his action prefiguring the Paschal supper when he will take bread and wine, give thanks, bless and then give them to his disciples with the directions: "Take and eat: This is my body. . . . Take and drink: This is my blood." These are the "rich food and choice wine" the prophet would describe for us in today's scripture reading. Both the miraculous meal provided on the mountain as well as the Eucharist are foreshadowing the joys of the eternal banquet which will be ours when Jesus comes finally in his glory.

Isaiah describes the action of God in dramatic strokes: ". . . he will destroy the veil that veils all peoples, the web that is woven over all nations." The veil, the intricate web that has been woven by a humanity fallen and separated from God, effectively excludes, ostracizes, walls off and buries whole segments of the human family, considering them as dead to God and to his people. Through the promise of Isaiah's prophecy God's people are called to reach out to embrace all who have been excluded from the God-chosen family circle, to be among that number of whom the one who is to come would be the Good Shepherd. No one is to be excluded from sitting at the dinner table of God's family, neither now nor in eternity. Every person is to be allotted their fair share of the bread from God's good earth as well as their invitation to feast on the Bread which has come down from heaven.

Today's Scripture Readings:

> *Isaiah 25:6-10;   Psalm 23:1-3, 3-4, 5-6;*
> *Matthew 15:29-37.*

Today's Advent Prayer:

> *"The Lord is my shepherd, my king, I shall not want." He leads me. He guides me. He feeds me.*

THURSDAY — FIRST WEEK OF ADVENT

Jesus Comes To Bring Us Home

Christmas is a traditional time for the gathering of family and friends. It is a time to reach out and touch the people we love. To be with them, in their company, that day is a treasured gift. Much detailed planning and coordination of travel arrangements, menus and holiday activities contribute to the experience of a joyful and memorable Christmas reunion. As the day draws near an anxious expectation begins to surface. There is an impatient anticipation of what is about to happen. A gnawing emptiness, a loneliness, grips the deep recesses of the hearts of loved ones aching to speed the arrival of long separated family and friends. There is warm pleasure in anticipating their coming, but there is pain in waiting for their impending arrival.

To know the experience of wanting to go home once again is to capture the spirit of this particular Advent day. There is a need for hope in the depths of every human being. It is a desperate experience to be marooned in a strange, inhospitable place, far from home. Dreams of happy memories which took place in familiar surroundings haunt the exile. Hopeless yearnings to see once again the never to be forgotten faces of long ago, to walk once more along well known and often traveled roads of former years, the wish to be at home once more can drive the exile to madness. Even the vaguest dream of returning home can turn plodding steps light, can cause an exile's heart to beat wildly.

That dream coming true is the precise experience portrayed by Isaiah in today's first scripture reading. He puts a song on the lips of an exiled people as they return home after the long, desperate, empty and lonely years of the Babylonian captivity. Their emotions surge as the city walls come into view. They are about to re-enter their holy city of Jerusalem, the city which historically held such a special place in the minds and hearts of God's people, that majestic city dominated by the magnificent Temple of Solomon standing high on the hill of Zion, a manifestation of God's continuous presence and care of his people. How much the exiles had hoped and dreamed of this day. Having faithfully trusted in God's unceasing care of them during their exile they now confidently call out to God to open the city gates in welcome for them, their song of wonder and joy culminating in profound adoration as they finally stand in the presence of him who had been an "eternal rock" for them during their painful years of captivity.

"Open to me the gates of holiness." From the profound depths of our spirits this Advent petition rises to harmonize with the song of God's people as they return home from exile. The only way to enter God's city now is by the way of the one who is coming to us, by way of Jesus who has described himself: "I am the way . . . I am the gate. Anyone who enters through me will be safe." The Lord is coming so that through him, the gateway, we might enter the City of God, the Kingdom of heaven, our Father's house. The sole means of entering there is through Jesus, the gate of the sheepfold. Apart from Jesus who is "the Way" there is no other way to go home. Any less complete acceptance of Jesus, no matter how noble, is totally inadequate. There is an urgent need, therefore, for him to come to us now. That need must be clarified in the profound depths of our spirit this Advent day. It should be the focus of our thoughts, our contemplation and our prayer.

To be welcomed into God's city requires more than mere desire, verbal acceptance or intellectual recognition of Jesus as "the way," "the gate." A profession of belief is inadequate. Faith must be kept. The Lord calls and challenges us to action: "None of those who cry out 'Lord, Lord,' will enter the kingdom of God but only the one who does the will of my Father in heaven." To do the will of another person is both a manifestation and a measurement of love for that person. Simply stated it is to be involved in a love affair with another. To do God's will is to love God — it is the equation of faith. Love is the distinguishing mark of the true disciple of the Lord. To love another person is to live with the spirit of that person. It is to breathe as one with them. It is to see things from their point of view, to act with wisdom. To live with the spirit of Jesus is the sole means of obtaining a welcome into God's City, to be accepted as an integral member of his family circle, to sit with him for an eternal banquet at the table in our Father's house.

Today's Scripture Readings:

> *Isaiah 26:1-6;   Psalm 118:1, 8-9, 19-21, 25-27;*
> *Matthew 7:21, 24-27.*

Today's Advent Prayer:

> *Come to me, you whom my heart loves.*
> *When you come may I hear:*
> *"Arise my beloved and come."*

FRIDAY — FIRST WEEK OF ADVENT

Jesus Comes To Let Us See

Isaiah's grand promise unquestionably must have sounded like a romantic poet's dream, seemed like a madman's raving to the exiled, enslaved, spiritless Hebrews in Babylon: ". . . out of gloom and darkness the eyes of the blind shall see." Freedom is promised to a depressed, hopeless people. Their fate is about to be radically transformed. They are going to be pardoned, redeemed. Chains shackling them in slavery will soon be torn away. Isaiah, God's spokesman, promises that the blindness of their black despair will be changed to a vision of light and hope by the touch of God's healing hand. They are promised: "Just wait! You'll see!"

To be in the dark, unable to see is a frustrating, confusing, frightening experience. In blind isolation a person can easily become disoriented and aimless. The breaking of dawn, the coming of light, gives hope. Blinded eyes see. Darkness and gloom are transformed by the wonder of light. It was the touch of God reaching through eternity that gave birth to light at the dawn of creation. God's touch continues to give light, vision and understanding to us in our time, in our human existence.

The blind men of today's gospel personally experience the wonder of creation as they receive their sight, the narrative unfolding very dramatically. Our attention initially is drawn to the repeated cries for pity surging from the pitch-black world of two sightless men. We see them lurching with groping, stumbling steps, even falling in their blinded, fevered pace, grasping out to each other for support in their efforts to capture the distancing Jesus striding along quickly well ahead of them. Using a familiar Messianic title, a recognition of Jesus' true identity, they plead with heartrending screams: "Son of David, have pity on us!" It was only when ". . . the blind men caught up with him," and encountered his question: " 'Are you confident I can do this?' . . . that he touched their eyes . . . and they recovered their sight."

Can we even imagine their experience of the explosion of light as their sense of sight suddenly comes to life? Can we suspect their wonder at seeing the face of Jesus for the first time as his hand draws away from his touch of their eyes bringing them the miracle of sight, followed by their first views of the world which had eluded their fullest experience, had laid in darkness, until this moment?

The blind men of today's gospel are you and me. They found Jesus, the person who described himself as "the light of the world," in their darkness. It is in that same darkness

where each of us will also find Jesus. The two men stumbling
after Jesus in their crazed search for light couldn't see him or
touch him. It was the Lord who reached out his hand to
touch them. With that touch they began to see, their total
existence changed. Their lives now pulsed with an unfamiliar force. They began to function from a totally new
vantage point as the veil of blindness lifted from their eyes.

Blindness is conquered by Jesus. "I am the light of the
world," is his self-description. He is still the "light of the
world." He would be our light now. We might say that he
holds light enclosed in his hand. As they groped in their
darkness to capture him in the gospel account so also do we
draw near to Jesus this Advent day in profound prayer,
stumbling in the darkness of our confusing ignorance. Like
blinded men we cannot approach him with any preconcep-
tions about him, even how he will respond to us. Our imagination is an obstacle; reasoning is a trap. They immediately
limit Jesus. Like the sightless men of the gospel we must
initiate any contemplation of the Lord by entering darkness
and a cloud of unknowing, the absence of knowledge that
lies between ourselves and him, if we are ever to be able to
see — know him, experience him, see him. Jesus holds the
blinding light of his divine personality and nature in the
hollow of his hand, to be seen or to be hidden as he wills to
open or close that hand in our presence. We approach the
mystery of the Lord, our Light, aware that he remains
hidden until he wills to reveal the reality of himself to us.
That is the wonder of seeing God for a moment. In that
fleeting experience of the gift of infused contemplation
ultimate reality is seen. The Lord is known. God is seen. It is
an unimagined blessing, an exploding bolt of light providing vision of the Divine, a foretaste of the Beatific Vision
experienced this side of eternity. Once seen so profoundly,
the blindness which is the natural lot of humanity here

on earth not only can be endured, but lived patiently in awe and reverence of our God until the Lord's final coming.

Today's Scripture Readings:

> *Isaiah 29: 17-24;   Psalm 27:1, 4, 13-14;*
> *Matthew 9:27-31.*

Today's Advent Prayer:

> *"Our Lord shall come with power, he will enlighten the eyes of his servants."*

SATURDAY — FIRST WEEK OF ADVENT

Jesus Comes To Establish His Kingdom In Us

As we come to the conclusion of the first week of our Advent preparation the faint melody and gentle questioning of a familiar Christmas carol emerge from the profound depths of today's scripture message:

> "Do you see what I see?
> Do you hear what I hear?
> Do you know what I know?"

"Do you see what I see?" We see the Lord approaching from afar with the desire to be an integral part of our existence. Like the dawn's light breaking through the darkness enveloping our world he comes to bring us home, to lead us to his kingdom. Isaiah announces that the steps taken through our life's journey should not be aimless wanderings because the Lord comes to lead us: "This is the way; walk in it." Desperate, hopeless tears of frustration or failure must never again be shed because we are assured: "When you cry out . . . he will answer you." The clear echo of a distant announcement is heard as a unique, unforgettable figure comes into view: "I am the good shepherd. I know my sheep and my sheep know me. My sheep hear my voice and they follow me." The Good Shepherd leads and feeds his sheep. He hears their cries and responds with healing and comfort. He cures them and gives them life.

"Do you know what I know?" Today's psalm praises the wonder of God's creative power, reminding us that in a continuous act of creation he never ceases touching what he has made, holding it in existence. "God looked at everything he had made and found it very good." If even for an instant he should forget what has come from his hand the creature would immediately become what it was before God made it; it would return to absolute nothingness. As a proof that the works of creation are not a mere process of mass production, that God is intimately and personally involved in the continued existence of every single creature, that God is not indifferent or neglectful of anything that he has created — the psalmist directs our attention to the stars of the galaxy. God knows everything he has made so perfectly, so intimately, so personally that he is portrayed as calling each of the myriad stars by name. If he responds so individually, so uniquely, to every star can there be any doubt about his continuous awareness of each one of us, knowing as we do that, of all the creatures on earth to which he has given existence, humanity alone was created to share an existence as members of his own family, to be his children? The time of Advent is a time of deepening wonder that our creator is coming to us. "The reign of God is at hand!"

"Do you hear what I hear?": "... no more will you weep. He will be gracious to you when you cry out, as soon as he hears he will answer you. The Lord will give you the bread you need and the water for which you thirst." Jesus proclaimed news that has clearly echoed through the ages. We hear it now: "The reign of God is at hand!" His announcement was not hollow and empty, made without the proof of evidence: "He taught in their synagogues, he proclaimed the good news of God's reign, and he cured every sickness and disease." He substantiated his claim with the witness of extraordinary works, the miraculous cures he performed.

"Will you do what I do?" Even in our day Jesus has compassion on all who grope and stumble through life handicapped by weakness, ignorance and blindness. For them he has commissioned each of us to be his disciple to announce the wonder of his reign to the people of our time. "The gift you have received give as a gift." That kingdom is clearly and authoritatively announced to the world's inhabitants by the response of faith demonstrated in the lives of those who profess to be believers. Those who meet us should be impelled to ask: "Let us walk with you because God is with you."

Today's Scripture Readings:

> *Isaiah 30:19-21, 23-26;   Psalm 147:1-6;*
> *Matthew 9:35-10:1, 6-8.*

Today's Advent Prayer:

> *"Let us see your face and we shall be saved."*

MONDAY — SECOND WEEK OF ADVENT

Jesus Comes To Set Us Free

In the course of their existence the Hebrew people frequently experienced national paralysis — immobility in the face of threatening annihilation by the overwhelming power of invading armies, the terror of violent persecutions resulting from their refusal to conform to the pagan values and practices of the nations surrounding them. In today's scripture reading Isaiah graphically recalls God's personal intervention in delivering them first from Egyptian slavery and centuries later from Babylonian captivity. The reminder of God's historical care of his people focuses attention on the wonder of the one who now comes to set us free.

Like the enslaved Hebrew nation we want to be free; we want to go home. Eyes blinded by the glamor of a dazzling, tempting, beguiling world want to see what is truly good, what will not corrode with time, what will be eternally desirable and satisfying, but what can never become boring because it will never be perfectly seen. Ears damaged by the rude clamor of a secular environment want to hear what is eternally truthful from one who speaks with a perfect love. Lame bodies and spirits want to jump with joy. Frightened hearts seek strengthening. Dumb lips want to speak with the one who has described himself as the "Truth." Weak and feeble, the parched land of human spirits wants to become fruitful: "Drop down dew you heavens from above."

> "They will see the glory of the Lord,
> the splendor of our God.

Strengthen the hands that are feeble,
> make firm the knees that are weak,
Say to those who are frightened:
> Be strong, fear not!
Here is your God,
> he comes with vindication;
With divine recompense
> he comes to save you."

The paralyzed man of the gospel is as good as shackled, tied down to his mat, incapable of walking free as a result of his paralysis. Totally dependent on friends, today's gospel describes the ingenious plan which allows the paralyzed man to be deposited directly at the feet of Jesus who entered his life with the startling command: "I say to you, get up!" With our own crippling disabilities it is not difficult for us to identify with the unnamed paralytic of today's gospel. Like him we want to be freed from those things which paralyze us, hold us down. For that to occur Jesus must come into our lives. Until we hear his voice, feel the touch of his healing hand, we will remain paralyzed, half dead, like the gospel paralytic.

The crippling, enslaving chains which bind us have been forged by sins of pride, passion and pleasure. With the paralytic we long to hear the liberating words: "My friend, your sins are forgiven you." The scribes and pharisees who were there rightly protested: "Who can do these things but God alone?" As we come weighted down, paralyzed with our sins, to our Advent encounter with Jesus in the Sacrament of Reconciliation we have the assurance that we will likewise hear: "I say to you, get up." As the restricting chains fall away through the words of sacramental pardon our spirits will join the gospel crowd in wonder: "We have seen incredible things today!"

The cure of the paralytic could not have occurred without his good "friends." They solicitously brought him to Jesus. This gospel detail should draw us to reflect on the meaning of friendship. "Friend" is a treasured title which cannot be conferred too easily. It is a revered title designating those select few who accept us just as we are, with all our paralysis. A friend is one who doesn't ask us to be any more than we are capable of being, not demanding that we conform to their notion of what we ought to be. Today we thank the Lord for the gifts of our friends. It is through them and their Christlikeness that Jesus reveals to us his care, his mercy, his patience, his pardon, his love, his forgiveness. In just those ways, like the friends of the gospel paralytic, our friends carry us into the presence of Jesus.

Today's Scripture Readings:

> *Isaiah 35:1-10;   Psalm 85:9-14;*
> *Luke 5:17-26*

Today's Advent Prayer:

> *"Our Savior is coming. Have no more fear."*

TUESDAY — SECOND WEEK OF ADVENT

Jesus Comes To Fulfill Promises

The Old Testament is an ongoing account of a history of rebellion by God's specially chosen people who with astounding frequency denied the binding terms of their covenant with God. They defied his majesty, presumed on his patience, rejected his rightful place in the fabric of their lives. They refused to trust him, defiantly disobeyed him who had created them as a nation, wondrously caring for them through the centuries, miraculously protecting and preserving them. Their infidelity resulted in punishment, God forgiving them after a period of atonement, returning them time after time to their previously favored status and care.

It is at one of those points of Divine forgiveness where we find this people in today's first scripture reading. Skeptical that God's care was sufficient to assure their safety and prosperity, they had placed their security in military alliances with the pagan nations surrounding them. This infidelity resulted in conquest by invading forces and the horrors of the Babylonian exile. But now through the prophet Isaiah, God reveals his love for them. They are reminded that they have not been abandoned, they are going to be rescued, "Comfort, comfort my people, says the Lord." God assures them of his enduring love for them.

It was a time for promises. "You are going home! Your fifty year exile is about to end! There's going to be another exodus and you'll be part of it! You are going to be rescued! Your freedom is imminent!" That's the good news which God's spokesman dramatically describes to God's people of the Babylonian diaspora in the scripture proclamation. The glory of the Lord is about to be revealed and everyone will see it. The road back home through the desert will be like a highway — there will be no terrors lurking, no perilous stretches to be traveled, no aimless wandering on this journey. The trip home will be direct, the road will be straight. His glory is about to be revealed. Everyone will witness that.

"Like a shepherd he feeds his flock;
        in his arms he gathers the lambs,
Carrying them in his bosom,
        and leading the ewes with care."

Now is the time for us to experience the fulfillment of
God's promises to us. As God did not forget his people, the
Hebrew nation, in their misery, God has not forgotten us in
our need for salvation. We hear a distant cry: "See, the Lord
is coming!" He is omnipotent, yet he reveals himself as a
shepherd, feeding his flock, gently caring for helpless
lambs. We are the sheep and the lambs. He is our shepherd.
He's coming now.

Today the psalmist invites us to sing with him a new
song to the Lord. He is a powerful king. We sing about our
king's glory, of him who rules with holiness, with love and
with patient mercy. We can hear all creation join in this
happy chorus of praise to God, the creator of all things. All
the people from every nation on every continent, the open
sea, the vast sky, the arid desert and the fruitful trees join in
giving praise to the approaching king.

"They shall exult before the Lord, for he comes;
        for he comes to rule the earth.
He shall rule the world with justice
        and the peoples with his faithfulness."

Our shepherd king neglects no one. He has a
shepherd's concerned care for every sheep in his flock, a
king's responsible awareness for every individual in his kingdom. Every stray, every wanderer is sought out, pursued,
searched for until found. Jesus, the Good Shepherd, invites
every single person, no matter how weak or wayward, to join
him on the highway back home to his Father's house.

The Lord shares his role with us: ". . . it is no part of your heavenly Father's plan that a single one of these little ones shall ever come to grief." We are reminded not to neglect our responsibility as parent, teacher, priest, bishop, brother or sister in Christ to one another. May no one suffer pain, be lost, damned, separated from God or come to any harm because of our irresponsibility. Through our concerned care may people experience the love, tenderness and forgiveness of Jesus.

When Jesus comes may he find us waiting, ready to welcome him as the dynamic integrating reality of our existence, guiding the direction and movement through each day of our life.

Today's Scripture Readings:

> *Isaiah 40:1-11;   Psalm 96:1-3, 10-13;*
> *Matthew 18:12-14*

Today's Advent Prayer:

> *"The day of the Lord is near: he comes to save us."*

WEDNESDAY — SECOND WEEK OF ADVENT

Jesus Comes To Re-Create Us

Can anyone imagine the blinding explosion of infinite power that accompanied the first creative act of God? Prior to the moment of creation there was only the eternity in which God existed. Everything else was endless nothingness. From that immeasurable void God called all created things into existence. The separation of light from darkness, the first act of creation, was literally a blinding explosion.

Creation is a divine action, a concrete statement of the infinite power of God. Only the creator can summon a creature to existence without using any material substance. The wonder of divine creativeness continues to be demonstrated — only God can keep his creation from returning to the utter emptiness from which it came unless he continuously wills it to exist. Creation, therefore is an ongoing action, a never-ending process of divine creativeness. Nothing in the universe, including ourselves, can exist without the continuous touch of the creative hand of him who first willed our existence.

Incapable as we are to imagine the first creative act, we are equally incapable of imagining the blinding explosion of Divine power in the wonder of re-creation necessitated by a defiant rebellion of his human creation. To heal the lethal effects of that revolt the Creator became personally present in his creation through his Incarnation, the sole participant of the work of re-creation in his redemptive action. God's creative power was shown to be greater than man's sins. He made his creation all over again.

We are confronted with the horror of the evil of sin, any sin: any crime of murder which was ever committed, any single abortion, even one misuse of the power of continuing his work of creation which he has shared with humanity and is degenerately used for self-pleasure in contraception, any calumny or detraction which has led its victim to mental breakdown or suicide, any instance of marital infidelity, the serious betrayal of a grave confidence by a trusted friend, any one human being dying of hunger when there is food produced and available from the bounteous earth, etc.! Any one of these instances is seen as seriously evil, gravely sinful. Take the whole catalogue which has been listed. Add to it all the sins you can think of. Multiply the result totalled by the number of sins in each category committed daily, annually, since the beginning of time: the number of adulteries, abortions, acts of terrorism and denials of God-given rights, since the dawn of creation. God's grace is greater than the sum total of all the sins ever committed.

The forgiveness of sin is re-creative. God's pardon is an act by which humanity is created all over again. His pardon is an eruption of power, as great and dramatic as his initial act of creation when he separated light from darkness. Humanity, which had severed its living bond with God, groaned in a world of chaos as it waited to be unchained and pardoned, redeemed so that it might be able to go home once again, to live in the presence of God. With the coming of the Lord, God became flesh, a work of re-creation was initiated. With the Incarnation light overcame darkness, life triumphed over death.

Our response to the touch of God's healing and creative hand, his redeeming pardon, is personally vocalized as we join in the song of the psalmist's poem:

> "Bless the Lord, O my soul;
>> and all my being, bless his holy name . . .
> He pardons all your iniquities . . .
>> He redeems your life from destruction."

Recognizing the gravity of a creature's rebellion we become slowly aware that God's grace is even greater. He reaches into the profound depths of our spirit to create us all over again. God's pardon is a creative act.

Advent is a time of waiting. Its weeks are days of mounting expectation for the Lord's coming. To wait with expectation for an extraordinary happening is to throb with hope. As the Holy One speaking through the prophet Isaiah exhorts his suffering, exiled people in Babylon not to lose faith in God's continued Divine care, we are likewise urged not to despair but to trust in God's promises, to await his coming with confident hope. As Isaiah brought the encouraging news that the people would soon return home, be re-created as a nation, strengthened to the extent that they would soar to the heights of national power, carried by God himself as on the strong wings of an eagle, so we are supported by promises of our creator whose nature makes him incapable of deception.

"Come to me, all you who are weary and find life burdensome, and I will refresh you" promises the Lord. "Take my yoke upon your shoulders." To experience the impact of Jesus' invitation we should know that a yoke is that part of the harness which couples together a team of draft animals, horses or oxen, in order that the heavy work of plowing or pulling a heavy wagon can be done more easily through the energy harnessed in their combined efforts. Jesus invites us to unite ourselves to him as we labor with the burdens of our human existence, to follow his lead, to walk at his pace, moving onward in cooperation with him, dependent on his presence, closeness and strength, always aware of our union with him.

A fear of a punishing, driving lash has no place in our relationships with God. The knowledge of our Father's love, his care, releases us from the awesome burden of rigid obedience which is motivated by fear of punishment. Our only fear should be to offend our Father who is infinitely good in his care of us, bountiful in his patience, loving and forgiving. That was the motivation of Jesus in responding to his Father. Jesus' yoke is that of a child's response to a loving father. "Your souls will find rest, for my yoke is easy and my burden light."

Today's Scripture Reading:

Isaiah 40:25-31;   Psalm 103:1-4, 8, 10;
Matthew 11:28-30.

Today's Advent Reading:

"Not according to our sins does he deal with us."

THURSDAY — SECOND WEEK OF ADVENT

Jesus Comes To Share The Joy Of His Father's Love

Advent prepares us for that extraordinary night when shepherds had visions and a virgin had a baby. It seems appropriate as we approach the mid-point of this preparation that in today's scripture readings God should speak to us about babies.

"You little monkey!" "Aren't you a rascal!" "Come here to me, you scalawag!" Using expressions like these parents have a fond way of tenderly and affectionately reaching out to squirming, precocious infants to pick them up, to cuddle them with the warmth and strength of their own bodies, to shower them with soft loving kisses. In today's first scripture text Isaiah portrays God whispering expressions of endearment to his people, calling them "worm Jacob" and "maggot Israel." God seems to cast aside his dignity, revealing himself as a Father whose love can never permit him to reject the offspring to whom he has given life even though the child may act with defiant rebellion. The pages of scripture provide undisputable testimony that God has repeatedly rescued his self-willed, disobedient children, his loved people, never abandoning them to the fate they create for themselves by their own actions, never alienating himself from them.

> "I am the Lord, your God,
>   who grasp your right hand,
> It is I who say to you, 'Fear not,
>   I will help you.'
> Fear not, O worm Jacob,
>   O maggot Israel;
> I will help you says the Lord."

Initiated with the birth of a child the bonding process is a significant moment in the development of a parental relationship with their child. Touching and speaking to the child is an important part of that process. Parents verbalize their hopes for their child. Frequently utopian dreams and unrealistic promises are whispered into the ear of their slumbering infant who is yet totally incapable of grasping the meaning or extent of what is being said. That is the precise scenario of today's scripture text from Isaiah. We should understand and appreciate it in that light. God describes what he will do for his beloved child, his special people. He sings a beautiful song about his plans for Israel: I will help you . . . be your redeemer . . . crush mountains for you . . . turn deserts into fertile farms, and forests for you . . . so that all may see and know that it was your God who has done this, created it. His promises defy the imagination, exceed any person's wildest dreams, reach beyond any child's realistic hopes. God proclaims his love for his offspring. The wonder of the Exodus was repeated for his people in the wonder of their later triumphant return to Israel from Babylonian captivity.

In our time the wonder of God's unreasonable, measureless love continues to repeat itself. Now we are the objects of his tender, loving mercy which knows nothing of limits or moderation. Love never counts the cost. Love impels toward results which are irrational, unexpected. "I the Lord will answer . . . I will not forsake them." We are preparing to celebrate the wonder of the event in which God became flesh, Divinity substantially united with humanity, so that he might do for humanity what it was incapable of accomplishing by its own efforts. God became intimately involved in a life giving relationship with his creature. Humanity would be substantially touched by the hand of its maker — recreated, made all over again, transformed by the personal involvement of its creator, present and active in throbbing human flesh at a particular moment in the calendar of time. These Advent days prepare us for the caring presence of God who comes to turn the reality of sin into a reality of holiness. "I will not forsake you," he now repeats to each of us personally: "I am the Lord . . . 'Fear not, I will help you.'" Today we are reminded that the Divine work of creation did not end when God rested on the seventh day after creating the earth and all it contains. The work of creation continues in our time as the redemptive hand of the Lord touches the humanity of each one of us.

A wild man from the desert dominates the Advent scene. He is John the Baptist announcing the beginning of a

new age. Striding toward us out of the pages of New Testament history we see the imposing figure of a man dressed in
animal skins, his hair untrimmed like that of a lion, the king
of beasts, his eyes bright, piercing, searing. Described by
Jesus as the last and greatest prophet he is God's fierce
messenger hurling a challenge to the people of his time as
well as to us today: "Prepare the way of the Lord." It was
John who introduced Jesus to the world by the use of a
mysterious title: "There is the Lamb of God."

Like Isaiah in the first scripture reading today Jesus
talks about babies in the gospel, explaining that any one who
belongs to God's family, even a person just emerging from
the life-giving waters of the womb of the baptismal font, is
greater than John the Baptist: "History has not known a
man born of woman greater than John . . . yet the least born
into the kingdom of God is greater than he." John is rightly
portrayed as a forceful man, physically strong, powerful
enough even to defy King Herod. Nevertheless the most
dependent member of the family of Jesus is stronger than
John and, shockingly, is capable of action even beyond the
ability of John. To be vitalized by the power of faith in the
Lord, to be inflamed with the light of gospel truth will result
in the formation of an individual more powerful than the
Baptist, the man divinely commissioned to prepare for the
drama of God's presence in time on the human scene.

"Even if you're a rascal, a rogue, I love you," God
assures us today. "You are my child. I'll always love you.
Know that for a fact. I'm your Father and I love you as a
father." That's God's announced commitment to us. We
must hear that, listen to it, accept it, live with it as a certainty.
The Lord we now wait to welcome will relay that reality to us
in the parable of the father who never wavered in the love
for his sons — one son rebellious and wandering, the other
unforgiving and vindictive. Their father went out to each of

them in turn, one to greet with welcoming embraces and kisses when he returns home penniless and in rags, reeking of the pig sty he tended to support himself after wasting his father's inheritance, the other to plead for an understanding of his father's indestructible love, his enduring forgiveness. Jesus' dramatic story exposed the fact that neither son really knew, actually understood, their father — his measureless love, patience and pardon. Today we are led to ponder the profound depths of our Father's love for us, to contemplate the fulfillment of a paternal promise.

Today's Scripture Readings:

> *Isaiah 41:13-20;   Psalm 145:1, 9-13*
> *Matthew 11:11-15.*

Today's Advent Prayer:

> *"Almighty Father, give us the joy of your love."*

FRIDAY — SECOND WEEK OF ADVENT

Jesus Comes, Welcome Him

John the Baptist preached a radical conversion to God, a response permitting neither hesitation nor compromise. Initially from his desert retreat and later from his station along the River Jordan his booming voice summoned everyone within hearing distance to a total turn-around in their lives. He called for an immediate and unconditional response to the reality of God and obedience to the clearly revealed will of God for his human creation in the conduct of their lives. John's own lifestyle provided concrete evidence of the degree of radical response sought in his preaching. One's answer to the summons for personal change demanded by his message was dramatically and decisively demonstrated by participation in the ritual of immersion in a purifying bath of baptism.

John was not universally accepted by his audience which rejected him as too austere, too unbending and rigid in his terms for conversion. These same people in turn dismissed Jesus as too soft with sinners, too indulgent in his lifestyle and scandalous in his association with persons like tax collectors, Hebrews who worked in cooperation with pagan Roman governors gouging the citizens with unjust taxations. They protested with sanctimonious indignation that Jesus was guilty of public scandal because he even ate with these tax collectors, defiling himself by association with these violators of the Law of Moses. They protested that John the Baptist would never participate in such shameful profane associations.

A frustrated Jesus challenged his accusers as pious frauds, hypocritical fault finders, impossible to please, difficult to satisfy because of their vacillating moods, their ambivalent feelings. He accused them of acting like spoiled, habitually ill-humored children. An enigma to him and to themselves, they haven't a notion of what they actually want. "We played you a tune but you wouldn't dance! We sang you a sad song but you wouldn't cry!"

The season of Advent is designed as an extended period of time to prepare ourselves to welcome the Lord Jesus into our lives here and now. He must be received just as he presents himself to us, just as he is. We need these Advent days to calm and open our spirits so that we will be able to listen closely and peacefully to what he will say and to remain objective in our judgment and acceptance of what he will do when he comes. We have to prepare ourselves during our Advent wait so that we will not demand that he be someone other than he is, someone more in conformity to our expectations, to our liking, constantly challenging or twisting what he teaches, demanding a message from him more in conformity, more palatable, to our taste and appetite. Nor can we play any hypocritical games with him when he comes. We prepare ourselves now to walk with him, the Lord, our redeemer, the Holy One, God with us, the light of our life.

He's coming now. He's drawing nearer. What's going to happen when he comes? A promise will soon be kept. From our experience we know that our anxiety level rises whenever we're about to come face to face with someone we anticipate will have a significant effect in our lives. For that reason it's consoling to hear the voice of God's spokesman, the prophet Isaiah, in today's first reading summarize for us what the person we're expecting is going to do when he comes. Isaiah is very specific. The Promised One is going to tell us what is essential for us to know. Our happiness hinges on what he is going to say. The successful fulfillment of the purpose of our existence hangs in the balance. His coming is crucial for us. He will not only tell us what we urgently need to know. He will lead us as well. Our existence will be essentially changed by his coming, surpassing our most extravagant, wildest imaginings, if we respond to him honestly, to the best of our ability. We will be the focus of his attention, the recipients of his care.

> "I, the Lord, your God,
>> teach you what is for your good,
>> and lead you on the way you should go.
> If you hearken to my commandments,
>> your prosperity would be like a river."

Today's Scripture Readings:

> *Isaiah 48:17-19;   Psalm 1:1-4, 6;*
> *Matthew 11:16-19.*

Today's Advent Prayer:

> *"We are waiting for our Savior, the Lord Jesus Christ;*
> *he will transfigure our lowly bodies*
> *into copies of his own glorious body."*

SATURDAY — SECOND WEEK OF ADVENT

Jesus Comes,
The Promised Savior

Today's scripture readings embrace a span of almost 1000 years. Ten centuries is a long time yet is negligible when compared to the eternity of God. Today's Advent spotlight is beamed on two figures, Elijah and John the Baptist, who share much in common though separated from each other by a thousand years.

Elijah suddenly appeared on the scene in scripture as a mighty prophet fearlessly speaking out in his divinely appointed task to turn the minds and hearts of the Israelites from their pagan ways back to covenant faithfulness. In fulfilling this mission he was hounded and persecuted, fleeing for his life as a result of violent threats against him. His entrance to the developing drama of God's relationship with the specially chosen people was without formal introduction or presentation of credentials. His role completed, he departed just as suddenly. His prophetic message was delivered as though from a flaming furnace. Clothed in the furry pelt of a bear, unquestionably he was an awesome man whose mission came to a dramatic conclusion when he was taken up, lifted out of the world in a fiery whirlwind. Through the centuries that followed, the sudden departure of Elijah was a source of much speculation concerning his eventual return to play a significant role in the start of the Messianic age with his introduction of the Promised One, the Anointed One, the Christ.

The dialogue recorded in today's gospel immediately followed the wonder of Christ's transfiguration where Elijah together with Moses was seen conversing with the Lord. When the disciples who had witnessed the extraordinary manifestation of Jesus' glory questioned him about Elijah's role in returning to open the curtain on the Messianic era, Jesus announced that the prophet had already returned in the person of John the Baptist who like Elijah had called for a change in men's hearts as well as their values, priorities and way of life. Like Elijah, John suddenly and without the formality of an introduction or presentation of divine credentials had commenced his role of preparing the people to welcome the Lord's coming.

John's was a powerful, commanding voice breaking the silence of the wilderness of an untamed world. "Prepare!"

he cried out then and cries now in our time. "I will lead you to him!" He will come if you are prepared, ready to receive him! As the world waited for the Promised One to come, we wait for him now to come to us personally. The silence of our bleak Advent is broken by a single booming voice. It is John the Baptizer. He shouts: "Prepare!"

> "Rouse your power
> and come to save us.
> Once again, O Lord of hosts,
> look down from heaven, and see . . .
> O Lord of hosts, restore us;
> if your face shine upon us,
> then we shall be safe."

In the depths of discouragement, fleeing for his life, unsure of the mission he had been given by God, Elijah fled to Mount Horeb in his search for God. He didn't find God in the mighty wind, a resounding earthquake or a raging fire. He found God, experienced the presence of God, in the whisper of a gentle breeze, a quiet breath. It is significant that in time John the Baptist would introduce God who became flesh, the Lord Jesus, not as a mighty figure but as a gentle lamb: "Behold the Lamb of God." If we are to find the Lord we can only meet him, experience him, in the same gentle way, in quiet darkness and in the peaceful silence of profound prayer.

Today's Scripture Readings:

Sirach 48:1-4, 9-11;   Psalm 80:2-3, 15-16, 18-19
Matthew 17: 10-13

Today's Advent Prayer:

> *"Lord, make us turn to you, let us see your face and we shall be saved."*

MONDAY — THIRD WEEK OF ADVENT

Jesus Comes, The Star Of David Draws Near

After forty years of desperate, confusing and often terrifying wandering through the Sinai desert the Israelite nation was assembled on the plain of Moab ready to receive the fulfillment of God's promise to Abraham that his descendants would be given a land of their own. Years of homelessness and hopelessness are now behind them. The desert experience has formed them as a nation and as a people of faith because of God's constant presence. Throughout their years of desert wandering, repeated infidelities were compassionately forgiven by God. He protected and cared for them in extraordinary, even miraculous ways, often lifting them from the depths of despair and guarding them from destruction at the hands of the ever threatening superior forces of the pagan armies through whose territory they passed. Now this wandering chosen people of God has come to the moment of posing a threat to others, competing with the Moabite nation for available land.

Today's scripture reading from the Book of Numbers describes the futile effort of the Moabite King, Balak, to call down evil on the threatening Israelites. He summoned Balaam, a practitioner of the mysterious art of casting spells, to call down a curse on them to weaken them, to render them powerless. However, as so often in the past, God intervened and guided the seer to deliver a blessing instead. The pagan Balaam was given a special gift, a charism, to be a spokesman for God to the Israelites. Balaam became an instrument in God's hands. That charism is described in the Book of Numbers:

> ". . . the spirit of God came upon him . . .
> The utterance of one who hears what God says,
>   and knows what the Most High knows,
> of one who sees what the Almighty sees,
>   enraptured, and with eyes unveiled . . ."

He predicts the coming of a king sometime in the future who will rule over this pilgrim people: "I see him, though not now; I behold him, though not near." Balaam is speaking of the Messiah. He makes a Messianic prophecy: "a star shall rule, a power shall rise." The promised Star of David is Jesus, who is called the Christ. Today the Christmas star is announced.

The Jewish priests and elders of today's gospel challenge Jesus' action of driving from the temple the thieving money changers and dealers offering unfit sacrificial animals for pilgrim worshipers. To his eyes it was an abomination to tolerate their continued presence within the sacred walls. Yet he was challenged: "On what authority are you doing these things? Who has given you this power?" The priests and elders themselves end up indicted as a result of their refusal to answer Jesus' reply to them, a challenge to their sincerity: "Was John sent by God?" Having abdicated their responsibility as religious leaders of the people by their denial of the clear-cut and demonstrated roles of both John the Baptist and Jesus as special representatives of God, the Lord's refusal to answer their challenge to him becomes an act of rejecting the authority of the priests and elders. The dynamics of this gospel text make it clearly apparent that they themselves have renounced their religious leadership of the people by their dishonesty in relating first to the Baptist and now to Jesus. This has resulted in the loss of their ability to discern where truth lies, where God's presence is to be found. There are disturbing implications here, frightening implications for anyone bearing the responsibility of a religious leader — bishop, priest, parent, teacher.

The pages of the Bible record an unfolding account of God's intervention in caring for his people as he guides them toward the fulfillment of his eternal plan. Scripture should be read as a dynamic revelation of God's caring presence and vital personal involvement in the lives of his people. In a hidden and mysterious way God has been present throughout the past history of his people. He has cared and still cares. He has been involved in the past and is involved still.

It is onto the stage of the present time that we now invite our God to step into the drama of our lives. With the psalmist today we pray for God's intervention. It is a prayer for deliverance.

> "Your ways make known to me . . .
> Teach me . . .
> Guide me . . .
> Pardon my guilt . . .
> Have pity on me . . .
> Take away all my sins . . .
> Rescue me . . ."

God's action of Incarnation and Redemption is only happening for us now. We are an integral part of the unfolding Divine plan. Today we look for him to come to us as he did to his people of old. As they once stood poised on the plain of Moab, now we stand poised waiting for him to come and touch our lives.

Today's Scripture Readings:

> *Numbers 24:2-7, 15-17;   Psalm 25:4-9*
> *Matthew 21:23-27*

Today's Advent Prayer:

> *"Your ways, O Lord, make known to me,*
> *teach me your paths,*
> *Guide me in your truth and teach me,*
> *for you are God my savior."*

TUESDAY — THIRD WEEK OF ADVENT

Jesus Comes
In The Precious Present

He's coming and he's coming soon! What kind of welcome does he expect from us? He wants a reception which clearly tells him that we trust him and that we are ready to listen to him with an open, responsive heart. His arrival should find us acting justly in our dealings with others and free from an idolatrous attachment to the things of the world. Our spirits soar with the awareness that his coming will result in the forgiveness of every single one of our personal sins. The prophet Zephaniah proclaims that consoling message of hope to people shamed at the recollection of their rebellious unfaithfulness: as God forgave his Chosen People of the Old Law he will forgive us now. His prophecy tells us to "take refuge in the name of the Lord." The past with its shameful memories will quickly recede into the shadows of divine forgetfulness as the "Light of the World" draws near: "On that day you need not be ashamed of all your deeds, your rebellious actions against me." The heightening expectation of his coming consoles us.

A vivid awareness of the Lord's approaching, tender touch is reinforced in the psalmist's poem today which directs our attention to the certainty that God watches over us, hears us and responds to us when we need his help. "The Lord hears the cry of the poor." He reaches out to protect us when we're threatened, rescues us when we're overwhelmed and comforts us when our hearts are broken.

> "I will bless the Lord at all times; . . .
> Let my soul glory in the Lord; . . .
> Look to him that you may be radiant with joy, . . .
> When the just cry out, the Lord hears them, . . .
> The Lord is close to the broken hearted; . . .
>   no one incurs guilt who takes refuge in him."

A contemplative monk once explained that the "Precious Present" is the only thing that should ever concern us because that's where we meet God. The person we're present to now, the task which now occupies our attention and energy, this precise moment in our existence should be our only concern. The past has gone by, the future has not come yet and in fact might never arrive. Where we are and what we're doing at the present moment is where God is met. Pleasing God, serving God can only be accomplished in the "now." Highly motivated plans for the future, vain imaginings, intensive and lofty theological speculation are not the contents of a relationship with God. They are dreams, only possibilities without substance. "Now" is the "Precious Present" where God is encountered.

God revealed himself as the Eternal Present to Moses on Mount Horeb when he described himself as "I AM" (Exodus 3:14). During his public ministry Jesus used precisely the same self-description to those who challenged him: "I solemnly declare it: before Abraham came to be, I AM" (John 8:58). In God there is no past, there is no future, there is no change. God is the Eternal Present.

For us to live in the "now" is to be absorbed in God. It is to be recollected. It is to be involved in a prayerful moment even while our attention might be absorbed in relating to another person or totally concentrated on the completion of a task. The "Precious Present" — that's the only place where we can be with God. That's how we'll be with God in eternity!

> "I will bless the Lord at all times;
>   his praise shall be ever in my mouth.
> Let my soul seek glory in the Lord."

Advent is a time of preparing for the coming of the Lord to us. Jesus himself has graphically described how our relationship with him in the "precious present" will determine our inheritance of God's kingdom:

> " 'Come. You have my Father's blessing! Inherit the kingdom prepared for you from the creation of the world. For

I was hungry and you gave me food. I was thirsty and you gave me drink. I was a stranger and you welcomed me, naked and you clothed me. I was ill and you comforted me, in prison and you came to visit me.' Then the just will ask him: 'Lord, when did we see you hungry and feed you or see you thirsty and give you drink? When did we welcome you away from home or clothe you in your nakedness? When did we visit you when you were ill or in prison?' The king will answer them: 'I assure you, as often as you did it for one of my least brothers, you did it for me.' " (Matthew 26:34-40)

Jesus comes to us in the "precious present" of people we see, or hear, or touch in our daily lives — the hurting, bruised, needy, scarred and bewildered people of the world of our day today, at this moment. In them we are to find Christ. In us they are to find Christ. The "precious present" is NOW.

In today's gospel parable Jesus is speaking about the "precious present" when he invites those who are accustomed to give mere lip-service to God to do two things. First he reminds us how detestable a pious fraud is to God, someone high on words but short on actions, someone who would project an image of doing the right thing but actually be a person who is self-willed, defiant and disobedient. Then he urges such a person to reform, to correct their ways. The Lord clearly tells us that we will not be welcomed into the kingdom of God because we had a lot of promise, because we were capable of doing virtuous and noble things, or because we had high hopes and great plans of responding obediently to God. Our entrance into the Eternal Presence, the glory of God, will be determined solely by our response to God in the "precious present."

Today's Scripture Readings:

> *Zephaniah 3:1-2, 9-13;   Psalm 34:2-3, 6-7, 17-19, 23*
> *Matthew 21:28-32*

Today's Advent Prayer:

> *"I will bless the Lord at all times . . .*
> *Look to him that you may be radiant with joy."*

WEDNESDAY — THIRD WEEK OF ADVENT

Jesus Comes To Touch Us

As a soft, gentle dew falls noiselessly in the night darkness and at dawn still clings to the bladed leaf, the holiness of God becomes present in a similar mysterious, silent way to touch our existence. Like a misty Spring rain falling from the heavens, permeating the earth, massaging dormant plants to life, divinity enters humanity, God comes to touch his creation, to bring it to life once again, unimaginably revitalizing it by his continued personal presence. The wonder of the Incarnation has resulted in the creative presence of God in our world, in our lives.

> "There is no just and saving God but me.
> Turn to me and be safe,
>   all you ends of the earth,
>   for I am God; there is no other! . . .
> To me every knee shall bend. . . ."

When the Lord became flesh and entered the human scene he didn't conform to the people's expectation about the promised Messiah. Today's gospel enables us to view Jesus through the eyes of John the Baptist. Momentarily we're shocked to realize that John is so confused and uncertain about the Lord's identity that he sent a delegation of his own followers to inquire directly from Jesus: "Are you the one we're waiting for — the one who is to come?" Obviously the pre-conceived notions of the Hebrews of the time regarding the Promised Messiah were shared by John. Jesus wasn't conforming to their expectations. He wasn't saying or doing what they expected the Messiah to say and do when he would finally arrive. Jesus wasn't as orthodox as the religious leaders anticipated, even demanded as a condition for acceptance. He wasn't organizing the expected extermination of the enemies of God and his special chosen people. He wasn't moving to fulfill the centuries old dream that the Messiah would establish them as a powerful, respected and feared nation. Jesus wasn't the temporal leader they had expected and consequently they were both disappointed and disillusioned.

Jesus responded to John's inquiry with his own question: "What are the facts?" And the facts provided vivid evidence to be relayed back to John by the messengers he had sent: "Go and report to John what you have seen and heard." The miracles he has performed provide indisputable testimony that he is the Promised One. His works, his actions, are his witness. They are the concrete evidence that God's hand has touched the world through him. They are creative actions demonstrating a special presence of the Divine — the blind recover their sight, cripples walk, lepers are cured, the deaf hear, dead men are raised to life. Those who are diseased, physically handicapped and even dead are changed by his presence, his word, his touch. He gives peace and healing, a new lease on life, to the bodies and spirits of hopeless people. The untouchables, the castoffs of society, the useless, even terrible public sinners not only hear the good news of God's love, but they bear the imprint of the fingerprints of God through the creative touch of being healed and pardoned by Jesus. His power is as obvious as the persons whose lives he has touched. There are none who are being excluded, none who are left out. The clearest sign of his messiahship is that the good news of God's care, compassion and pardon is experienced by all — the devout Hebrew and the superstitious Gentile, the terrible public sinner, the despairing parent, a little child — "the poor have the gospel preached to them." Such a Messiah was not expected then and for that reason he was a scandal when he came.

For some people, even among those who would consider themselves people of faith, Jesus is a scandal now because he won't conform to who should be included in the embrace of his caring arms and who should be left out. "Blest is the man who finds no stumbling block in me."

The Lord's coming is the focus of our Advent — his coming at birth to Bethlehem, his coming in grace to each of us personally here and now, and his future coming at the end of time. The holiness of God dropped down like gentle rain, silently and mysteriously entering the human experience by his Incarnation. With human flesh received in the womb of Mary he brought the very holiness of God to humanity, eventually invading the stronghold of death, breaking it open and scattering its dark treasure. Though his body was swallowed by the earth in burial, with his resurrection it was released from death so that he might share that new life with a newly created humanity. His body sown in the earth like a buried seed sprang from there to yield a harvest of people raised from spiritual death. Salvation budded forth from his opened grave.

Jesus didn't come to the world at his Incarnation with wrathful judgment, nor does he come to us now in that way. He still comes with healing and a blessing to those who need him. He still comes as a creative presence to each of us. He still comes, touching us not like a violent storm but as a gentle morning dew falling, creating peace in the depths of our spirits.

> "Let Justice (holiness) descend, O Heavens, like dew
>   from above,
>   like gentle rain let the skies drop it down.
> Let the earth open and salvation bud forth;
>   let justice (holiness) also spring up!
> I, the Lord, have created this."

Today's Scripture Readings:

Isaiah 45:6-8, 18, 21-25;   Psalm 85:9-14
Luke 7:18-23

Today's Advent Prayer:

*"Let the clouds rain down the just one,
and the earth bring forth a savior."*

THURSDAY — THIRD WEEK OF ADVENT

Jesus Comes,
A Gift Of God's Love

They were once God's specially loved people. Now they are captive and exiled, lonely and depressed, rootless and pained, abandoned and hopeless, slaves in a foreign land. The people are far from home, spirits growing ever weaker as their memories fade of the peaceful, happy years they once lived in their own land. The anguish of their present condition in life becomes more and more severe with the realization that their situation can be blamed on no one but themselves. It is a consequence of their own foolishness. Above all the nations that ever existed on the face of the earth they were God's special people and they had disregarded him, forgotten his concerned care for them, his patience with them throughout the history of their relationship with him. They rejected his love. They were no better than an adulterous spouse.

Driven by worldly desires, motivated by secular values, guided by their fantasy of becoming a great national power they arrived at the point where they refused to trust in God's historical extraordinary care of them as his unique spouse. Their leaders not only formed military alliances with neigboring pagan nations but even permitted the introduction of idolatrous worship and pagan customs into the land and lives of God's chosen people. Abandoned by God to their human designs, eventually they were conquered by the mighty military power of Babylon. Capable leaders, skilled artisans, educated youth, the cream and hope of the nation were led off as captives, leaving behind a devastated landscape, a destroyed holy city of Jerusalem, their temple a smoking ruin. The unfaithful spouse was banished. The Babylonian captivity had begun.

After seventy lonely years of exile the people can't believe it when from God's spokesman, the prophet Isaiah, they hear a joyful song revealing God's continued love for them — that he's willing and anxious to embrace them once again as his beloved spouse:

> "For he who has become your husband is your Maker;
>   his name is the Lord of Hosts;
> Your redeemer is the Holy One of Israel,
>   called God of all the earth,
> The Lord calls you back,
>   like a wife forsaken and grieved in spirit,
> A wife married in youth and then cast off,
>   says your God.
> For a brief moment I abandoned you,
>   but with great tenderness I will take you back.
> In an outburst of wrath, for a moment
>   I hid my face from you;
> But with enduring love I take pity on you,
>   says the Lord, your redeemer . . .
> My love shall never leave you. . . ."

Today's psalm captures the response which Isaiah's message triggered in the people who heard his announcement: "You changed my mourning into dancing." Shocked to learn of God's unimagined pardon and consoling love, defying their wildest dreams, they display their wonder and joy. The weight of heavy hearts removed, they now dance with abandon, carefreely, in light, youthful steps. They burst with the expectation of the fulfillment of their lover's promises. Once again their hearts throb with hope. They are to be freed. They have every reason to sing and dance. They are ecstatic. They will be going home again.

Advent is a time of hope for us. It is a season of promise and expectation. As the Lord once came to a world waiting for the Promised One he now comes to us. In today's gospel he asks us a piercing question: "Have you found what you've been looking for?" He tells us not to be satisfied with what can only give temporary satisfaction, momentary distraction. Don't be content with a desert illusion, a mirage, a figment of imagination, something as insubstantial as crystallized breath on a frosty morning.

Advent is the time to reach out expectant, desirous hands to receive a wrapped up gift which is offered to us. The gift is the Person of God wrapped in human flesh. A gift packaged like that is the sure way a human can concretely know divine love and mercy. God manifests his tender care, his compassionate pardon, the wonder of his love in the Word made flesh. There isn't a person who cannot understand such a gift.

God gives the gift of himself. He will fulfill the promises of the prophets and the fullness of the Law by his personal involvement in the action of redeeming us. God and his love are not illusions. This Advent day should help us grow in that awareness.

Today's Scripture Readings:

> *Isaiah 54:1-10;   Psalm 30:2, 4-6, 11-13*
> *Luke 7:24-30*

Today's Advent Prayer:

> *"For a brief moment I abandoned you,*
> *but with great tenderness I will take you back.*
> *In an outburst of wrath, for a moment*
> *I hid my face from you;*
> *But with enduring love I take pity on you,*
> *says the Lord, your Redeemer."*

FRIDAY — THIRD WEEK OF ADVENT

Jesus Comes, And He Is God

It seems that today's gospel episode can be best appreciated when it is viewed as taking place in a courtroom setting. Because he had spoken of God as his own father Jesus is immediately confronted with a public challenge by the Jewish leaders. His statement clearly implied his equality with God. Therefore, indicted on the charge of blasphemy, he is instantly put on trial and required to produce witnesses to substantiate the implications of divine equality.

We are active participants in this courtroom drama. We are more than mere onlookers, spectators, an audience of impartial observers insulated from sharing in the process from the safety of seats in the visitor's gallery. None of us can sit on the sideline during this trial. Each of us sits as a member of the jury carefully hearing, evaluating, weighing the evidence Jesus presents in his defense. It is urgent that

we responsibly fulfill our role — listening closely, giving
utmost attention to every point of testimony so that we will
be able to reach a just verdict in his case. The scene enacted
reaches beyond the person who has been indicted. The
decision to be made is a matter of life or death for each of us
personally. Our acceptance or rejection of Jesus hangs in the
balance.

To defend and justify his claim that he is God's Son, the
one who does his Father's work, Jesus calls on reputable
witnesses for testimony. John the Baptist, the first witness
summoned, is an accepted, an accredited witness even by
those who have brought the charge of blasphemy against
Jesus. They have recognized John as a prophet, a
spokesman, a voice for God in their time. Jesus reminds
them that they have received positive, supporting testimony
on his behalf from John. The Baptist was the one who
prepared the people for his appearance on the scene. Jesus
reminds his accusers that when the Pharisees and Sadducees
sent the priests and Levites to question John and ascertain
his role they were told by the Baptist, quoting Isaiah: "I am
'a voice in the desert, crying out: Make straight the way of
the Lord!' " (John 1:23; Isaiah 40:3)

The second substantial piece of evidence which Jesus
presents in his defense are the extraordinary things he has
publicly done. His miraculous works are clear testimony that
he has a vital bond with God. Unless he had come from the
Father he could never have been able to perform such
wonders. His works speak for themselves. They are his
witnesses, each miracle a living demonstration of his power,
of his identity:

> "These very works which I perform
> testify on my behalf
> that the Father has sent me."

His case abruptly rests. The decision is left in our hands, the members of the jury. Now it is our decision to make. Do we accept Jesus as divine or not?

Today the neatly packaged gift offered to us yesterday begins to be unwrapped. The gift is ours to take. Our experience as jurors today has offered us a clear-cut look at the person of Jesus who is the gift extended to us. Beneath the wrappings of his humanity we are given a glimpse of his divinity. Without any doubts we know the nature of the person who is coming to us. The gift given to us is God himself. Suddenly numbed with amazement at the gift put into our hands, our hearts soar with joy and gratitude.

Isaiah is a prominent figure on our Advent stage today. To prepare for his coming, his involvement in the fabric of our lives, God speaks to us now through his spokesman, the prophet Isaiah. To grasp the impact and scope of the message communicated to us we should be aware that as Isaiah fulfills his prophetic office he is increasingly overwhelmed at the measureless distance between the holiness of God about whom he speaks and the awful sinfulness of the humanity to whom he brings God's message. Today's scripture reading reveals that the holiness of God is about to be experienced in the world, that redemption is about to become a reality.

From our perspective, our place in the history of Christianity these are understandable, acceptable notions, but can we grasp with any degree of clarity and appreciation how disturbing, how mysterious, this message was for the audience who heard the prophecy some seven centuries before its fulfillment with the events of the Incarnation and Redemption? Our Advent experience should include the wonder of anticipating and impatiently desiring the coming of the Promised One who is the very holiness of God.

".... my salvation is about to come,
    my justice (holiness) about to be revealed . . .
Let not the foreigner say,
    when he would join himself to the Lord,
    'The Lord will surely exclude me from his people.'
The foreigners who join themselves to the Lord, . . .
Loving the name of the Lord,
    and becoming his servants —
All who . . . hold to my covenant,
Them I will bring to my holy mountain
    and make joyful in my house of prayer; . . .
For my house shall be called
    a house of prayer for all peoples."

God promises a vital, throbbing existence in his presence — knowing him, worshiping him, contemplating him as he is. He speaks of a happiness unknown this side of eternity, to be experienced by "foreigners," non-Hebrews. Participation in Messianic salvation is offered to all who have faith in the Lord, accepting him as savior, guiding the conduct of their lives by his revelation, his covenant commandments. No one is excluded — not one of us. All humanity is offered an invitation to join their voices with the eternal song of praise by the blessed before the face of God.

"O God may all the people praise you." We join the psalmist in a prayer responding to the reality of God who has become flesh. He is eternal and perfect, creative and all holy, infinitely forgiving, possessing the fullness of love. We bless him for who and what he is. We accept him now as he personally comes to us at this moment of our existence. We seek his blessing, ask him to be patient with our blindness and hesitation in completely welcoming him as our Lord, God with us. We praise and thank God for what he has done for us. We are embarrassed at the realization that we have been so unfeeling and indifferent to the presence of God to us in the person of Jesus both now and in the past. We sing the psalmist's song to the Lord:

> "May God have pity on us and bless us;
>   May he let his face shine upon us.
> So may your way be known upon earth;
>   among all nations, your salvation.
> May the nations be glad and exult . . .
>   the nations on the earth you guide.
> The earth has yielded its fruits;
>   God, our God, has blessed us.
> May God bless us,
>   and may all the ends of the earth fear him!"

Today's Scripture Readings:

> *Isaiah 56:1-3, 6-8;   Psalm 67:2-3, 5, 7-8*
> *John 5:33-36*

Today's Advent Prayer:

> *"God, our God, has blessed us."*

DECEMBER 17

Come, Wisdom Of God

The family roots of Jesus are uncovered in today's gospel. His genealogy reveals that he is not only a son of Abraham, but also a descendant of the royal line of David. Jesus has the blood of kings in his veins. The Advent curtain opens wider for us today permitting us to see the family tree of Jesus, a necessary view so that we can become better prepared for the event of his birth at Bethlehem which we'll be celebrating within the week.

"Joseph went from the town of Nazareth . . . to David's town of Bethlehem — because he was of the house and lineage of David — to register with Mary, his espoused wife, who was with child." (Luke 2:4-5)

Today's reading from the book of Genesis proclaims the promise of kingship made to Judah by his father, Jacob, a promise to be fulfilled almost 2000 years later in the one to be recognized in time as the King of Kings, the Lord Jesus, the direct descendant of Judah and most especially of David, Israel's greatest king, as recorded in the gospel genealogy. These scripture readings are of awesome power and impel us by their content toward the Christmas celebration. They are a necessary revelation to us if we are to participate in the wonder of the coming of the Lord Jesus into our world in the event of his Incarnation, as well as his coming to each of us personally at this moment in time.

Matthew begins the story of Jesus Christ with a list of his ancestors. The lengthy genealogy of Jesus is a sobering reminder that the script of the drama of our redemption was written from eternity in the halls of heaven, scheduled to be played according to God's timetable. The lengthy list of mostly unfamiliar names in the genealogy shouldn't bore us and must not result in our impatience because it gives us an opportunity to glimpse God's long range plan for our redemption, offering us an unexpected vision of the reality of his eternal love for us. There isn't a person among those listed on the family tree of Jesus who is unimportant or insignificant, a reminder of our importance in God's creative and redeeming plan. No matter how weak or sinful they might have been, God was not moved to close the

curtain on the drama of his redeeming love. Our spirits lift
and we are strengthened in our awareness of that fact. The
gospel genealogy today impels us toward the Christmas
celebration, the coming of Jesus to the world then and his
coming to us now.

The roots of Jesus' family tree are blemished, gnarled
and scarred. It is not a pretty picture. His genealogy was
composed of individuals who were an odd assortment. It
begins with a deceptive, calculating Jacob who stole a birth-
right. His offspring, Judah, negotiated the sale of his own
brother into slavery. As the list of ancestors begins it is
immediately obvious that God frequently does not select the
holiest, the best or the noblest of persons to participate in
the fulfillment of his plans. The stock from which Jesus
descended included idolaters, murderers, power seekers
and self-indulgent rogues. King David, a significant individual on the family tree was a stunning blend of saint and
sinner, a pious but corrupt monarch, capable of creating
profound spiritual poems and equally capable of engineer-
ing murder so that he could marry the wife of his victim. For
the most part the final segment of the genealogy from the
Babylonian captivity to the arrival of Jesus as the Messiah is a
collection of people who can be best described as unknowns.

A special notice should be taken of the five women
named in the genealogy. One was a seducer, another was a
prostitute, the third was a foreigner, not even a Hebrew, and
the final Old Testament woman on the list was an adulteress.
Scandalous and justly held in scorn, we are sobered by the
realization that they were instruments in God's hands, each
with a significant and necessary role to play in continuing
the family line which produced the Messiah. These four
women serve to introduce the fifth woman named in the
genealogy, Mary the wife of Joseph, the instrument of the
Holy Spirit who gave flesh to the Son of God in her womb,
Jesus called the Christ.

The genealogy is actually only the beginning of the story of Jesus Christ. The narrative continues in our time and contains a similar assortment of individuals — unknowns, insignificants and people who are unimportant, saints and sinners — each of us playing a major role on the stage of Christianity. The proclamation of the genealogy in today's Advent liturgy encourages us as we wait for the Lord's coming to us now. As the vital touch of others, many of them unknown, has brought us to the experience of faith so do others depend on our touching them so that they also might become part of the story of Jesus.

We join our voices in reverent prayer with that of the psalmist in a song to a newly crowned king who is a true descendant of David and not a usurper. His reign will produce peace and holiness for his people. He will reach out in care for the afflicted and poor. Jesus is that ideal king. His arrival will soon be announced by the song of heavenly messengers: "Glory to God and peace to men." Today's psalm reveals that the reign of the new king will not be confined to a particular time or place, age or continent. His rule will be universal: "All the tribes of the earth shall be blessed." We pray: "May he rule from sea to sea." His reign will be eternal, "till the moon be no more." The psalm joins the gospel genealogy in impelling us toward the Christmas celebration.

Today's Scripture Readings:

> *Genesis 49:2, 8-10;   Psalm 72:3-4, 7-8, 17*
> *Matthew 1:1-17*

Today's Advent Prayer:

> *Today the Church, a caring and loving mother, introduces*
> *us to an intensive program of immediate preparation for our*

participation in the wonder of the Lord's coming. Simply presented as a short prayer before the gospel each day from now until Christmas eve we will be guided step by step eventually to stand before him in awesome wonder when he arrives. Christmas should be a profound experience and each of these daily prayers, the Alleluia antiphons, develops the extraordinary vision we need for such an experience. Each one of these antiphons merits a special focus in our Advent prayer, our meditation and contemplation.

We pray today:

> *"O Wisdom of our Lord most high,*
> *guiding creation with power and love:*
> *Come, teach us to walk in the paths of knowledge."*

A special gift from God, knowledge destroys ignorance and equips a person with an instinctive reflex to recognize and respond to the inherent emptiness of each and every creature, the futility of giving them any more value than they are worth. To have knowledge is to possess the science of the saints, to hold the ingredients, to have the recipe of a holy life. The knowledge described is far more than knowing facts, possessing data. It is a unique gift enabling us to recognize the intrinsic worth of things, the sheer uselessness of giving them any more value than they should have — wealth, status, power, possessions, titles, positions, physical beauty, intellectual ability, the admiration of other people. The knowledge sought will enable us to pass judgment on the world and all it contains, creatures which are always attractive and often deceptively alluring.

"To walk in the paths of knowledge" we must be able to see things from God's point of view. To do that the very spirit of God is needed, literally to be guided by God's presence. We

need wisdom, the greatest gift that God can share with us. To possess such a gift is to be able to rise above folly, to contemplate divinity. Precisely, that will occur when we see the Lord who comes to us, God who has become flesh. Therefore all day today we profoundly pray:

> "O Wisdom of our God most high,
> guiding creation with power and love:
> Come, teach us to walk in the paths of knowledge."

DECEMBER 18

Come, God With Us

The drama of the Incarnation was played on the stage of history in many acts and scenes over the course of centuries involving a huge cast of players, many of them with starring roles. It is unfortunate that the limitations of our humanity do not permit us to completely grasp in a single instant all the dynamic details of the unfolding reality of God becoming flesh in our experience of celebrating the Christmas event which is now approaching us so quickly. Like a mother who knows the limitations of her children only too well, the Church today begins to prepare us in a very special way for our participation in the event of God coming to his people.

The clear, resonant voice of Jeremiah the prophet echoes through the ages announcing the person we are preparing to welcome into our world, into the reality of our existence:

> "Behold, the days are coming, says the Lord,
>   when I will raise up a righteous shoot to David;
> As king he shall reign and judge wisely,
>   he shall do what is just and right in the land."

Naming him "The Lord our justice," Jeremiah focuses attention on the holiness of the king as his predominant characteristic. The prophet describes a future king whose holiness will bring him to rescue those who are suffering, those who are confused and aimless in their lives, those in need. God's people will be saved and live in security because of the promised king's holiness. The world will experience the reality of his glory. Jeremiah's description of the king to come as a "righteous shoot" is heard throughout the remaining pages of the Old Testament as a classic description of the Messiah, a king who will be totally different from the weak, rebellious, sinful kings beginning with David, a powerful king of the people of God, of Judah and Israel. The royal dynasty of David will be restored perfectly by Jesus who will rule with holiness, sensitivity, gentleness, wisdom and righteousness. In time we will come to recognize our king as the Good Shepherd and the King of Kings.

David himself invites us to join in his psalm today, a royal song to our anointed king of the house of David. It is a song proclaiming the holiness of our king, most especially the sanctity demonstrated in his tender, concerned care for his people. He has pity on them. He rescues them.

> "Justice shall flourish in his time,
> and fullness of peace for ever."

It should be noted that in scripture the words "holiness" and "justice" are synonymous. The terms are interchangeable. The Lord Jesus himself used the terms in such a way in his Sermon on the Mount: "Blessed are they who hunger and thirst after justice (holiness), they shall have their fill." (Matthew 5:6)

As the days evolve between now and our celebration of the Lord's Nativity on Christmas Day a major person in the immediate unfolding of the drama of God's redemptive plan will be introduced to us each day, to stand momentarily on the Advent stage in the beam of history's spotlight. Each one will fulfill a significant and necessary role in the developing account of God becoming flesh.

Joseph, the husband of Mary, plays that starring role today in the script of the Incarnation, pausing briefly for the narration of today's gospel text but soon stepping back into the shadows of the stage, not leaving a word recorded for posterity. What has been recorded about him however is significant. We should study it closely today. It provides priceless personal direction for our Christmas preparation and celebration.

Yesterday's detailed genealogy which uncovered the roots of Jesus' family tree is continued and completed by Matthew's gospel text today. The genealogy of the Lord reached its apex with the identification of Jacob the father of Joseph. "Jacob was the father of Joseph the husband of Mary. It was of her that Jesus who is called the Messiah was born." Today's gospel makes it obvious for us why God selected Joseph for such a vital role in the redemptive plan. The selection embraced far more than that Joseph was of the genealogical family of David, a fact confirmed by the angel Gabriel who addresses Joseph in today's gospel text as "Son of David."

When we think of the annunciation we are accustomed to recall the dramatic sequence of verbal exchange between God's messenger, the angel Gabriel, in his appearance to Mary and the wonder of her role in conceiving and bearing a son to be called Jesus, as that event is described by St. Luke (Luke 1:26-38). However, today St. Matthew lets us witness a much different encounter between that same angelic messenger, Gabriel, and Joseph the husband of Mary in another annunciation. These are complementary accounts which confirm the gift of freedom which God offers to every single person, both then and now, relative to their participation in the wonder of God's plan of salvation. All the details of one's involvement might not be spelled out, but no one is ever duped by God to become an unwilling participant in his saving action.

Joseph is disturbed. The fact that the annunciation to him occurs by means of a dream perhaps reflects that he has been experiencing many disturbing dreams since learning of Mary's pregnancy. It is a fact that he is Mary's husband. In the custom of the times he and Mary had legally contracted marriage before witnessess some time before, but in the interim period between the age of puberty when the marriage contract was made the couple continued to live apart in their own parents' homes until the husband was able to provide a home for his wife and to support her. During that time intercourse was not permissible. Now Joseph is disturbed at Mary's apparent scandalous pregnancy. What was he to do?

Up to the moment of Gabriel's announcement Joseph had no knowledge of the divine origin of Mary's child. The angel communicated God's plan to Joseph including both the conception and future of the child. Described by Matthew as an "upright man," a just man, Joseph accepted God's revelation and accepted Mary's child as his own. Such acceptance was all that was necessary for legal paternity. He acknowledged the child as his, thereby becoming the child's legal father, more than a foster father.

It is obvious why Joseph was chosen by God for such a role. An "upright man," he conformed to the Law of God, he measured up to the Jewish standard of holiness. He was sensitive to the sanctity of marriage as required by God's law and he was conscientious in protecting other people. He was disturbed by Mary's pregnancy but did not become self-righteous at Mary's apparent public disgrace. He was concerned about protecting her. Joseph, the observer of the Law, called to share so intimately in the fulfillment of God's plan of redemption, can justly be addressed as: "Saint Joseph."

Today's Scripture Readings:

> *Jeremiah 23:5-8;   Psalm 72:1, 12-13, 18-19*
> *Matthew 1:18-24*

Today's Advent Prayer:

> *"All this happened to fulfill what the Lord had said through the prophet:*
>
> > *'The Virgin shall be with child*
> > *and give birth to a son,*
> > *and they shall call him Emmanuel',*
> > *a name which means 'God with us.' "*
>
> *It is significant that the closing verse of Matthew's gospel should contain the fulfillment of the name "Emmanuel": "Know that I am with you always, until the end of the world." (Matthew 28:20)*
>
> *Jesus is totally different from any king which the world had ever experienced, and in fact even expected. He is "God with us." As he came once we invite him, we beg him, to come now once again to us personally. We need him to stretch out his*

mighty hand to touch our lives, to become present to us. We ask him to free us from the malice and consequences of our sins and to fill us with the light of knowledge, understanding and wisdom which will enable us to live with future faithfulness.

The power of God in the person of Jesus, Emmanuel, God with us, comes now to rescue us. God personally comes to lead us home.

Today a profound prayer rises from the depths of our being:

> *"O Lord,*
> *Leader of ancient Israel,*
> *giver of the Law to Moses on Sinai,*
> *rescue us with your mighty power."*

DECEMBER 19

Come, Flower Of Jesse

Our full attention today rivets on a scenario unfolding on the Advent stage which embraces a span of more than twelve centuries. The movement of a cast of ordinary people like ourselves performing the familiar tasks of everyday life comes to a frozen halt with the appearance of mysterious ambassadors. Angels sent by God from the halls of heaven announce to the wife of Manoah in today's first scripture reading and then to Zechariah in the gospel account that the life-long, hopeless, barren shame of their marriages would soon end by the birth of sons, Samson and John the Baptist. The parents are told that their sons will be uniquely consecrated to God. They will belong totally to God so that each of them might perform a special service. Their commitment by Nazarite vow will be their source of strength enabling them to fulfill the difficult task of their divine commissions. No details are provided to the parents relative to the particular roles which their sons are to perform.

These angelic appearances are manifestations of God's personal, active involvement in a plan designed from all eternity, a plan not to be frustrated even by the natural limitations of the normal years of child bearing. We recognize that the angelic messengers to whom those missions have been entrusted are creatures of God whose nature is superior to the humans to whom they come and that their superior dignity is appropriate to the perfection of the one they represent. The ambassador's presence is as good as the presence of the one who sent them; it is as if God himself had come to tell the wife of Manoah and Zechariah the wonder he was about to perform for them. God is at work. He intervenes in a special way. It is a sign for us of God's constant action in the universe and in the lives of the men and women he has created.

God works miracles to fulfill his promises. Today's scripture readings announce what God can do — that Samson in the early history of God's people and then John the Baptist more than a thousand years later were unique gifts to the world by God himself. Their appearance in the course of human history, in the unfolding of the Advent account was a special divine action. Samson and John are to be special instruments, charismatic leaders, used to deliver God's people from paganism, idolatry and an unfaithful philosophy of life. Each of them was consecrated from birth to perform a unique, special service for God: Samson to deliver Israel from the overpowering domination of the Philistines, John to play the major role of immediately preparing humanity for the redemption to be accomplished by God who was becoming flesh.

The divine ambassadors speak in turn to the wife of Manoah standing to one side of the Advent stage today and then to Zechariah on the opposite side. We should note that the implementation of God's plan of salvation was appropriately announced to Zechariah in the Holy Place, the actual location of God's presence to his people in the Temple of Solomon at Jerusalem. Hesitant and fearful, Zechariah challenges the angel God has sent to him, unable to accept the message with trust in God's care and providence. He doubts because he hasn't been provided with all the answers. His response is a vivid challenge to us that it is possible even to perform the most profound works of religion as occupied Zechariah in the Holy Place and still lack a basic trust in God. As the curtain falls in today's tableau, Zechariah is left standing speechless on the Advent stage. Significantly the name "John" was given by Gabriel to Zechariah — even before the conception of the child — to signify that God had a special role in the work of salvation for this child of promise. Only when the name was conferred on his newborn son was Zechariah's power of speech restored to him.

Each of us turns mute, speechless, too overwhelmed for words, by the developing awareness of God's personal touch in our lives. Like Zechariah and the wife of Manoah none of us is too old, too weak, too insignificant to be an integral part of God's saving plan. Today's liturgical scenario impels us to welcome the touch of God's creative hand in our lives. We are motivated to change our habit of holding God at a distance, keeping him at arm's length. How easy it is to glibly profess our lives for God, to boast of our faith as long as nothing is asked of us personally or as long as we keep God far enough away from us that we are unable to clearly hear his voice. But we draw close enough to God now that we might hear his reply to the prayer we make in unison with the psalmist — a promise to trust and a plea to be set free:

> "For you are my hope, O Lord;
>   My trust, O God, from my youth.
> On you I depend from birth;
>   from my mother's womb you are my strength."

Today's Scripture Readings:

> *Judges 13:2-7, 24-25;   Psalm 71:3-6, 16-17*
> *Luke 1:5-25*

Today's Advent Prayer:

> *The genealogy of Jesus reveals that he is a descendant of David, the youngest son of Jesse, who was personally selected by God to become the powerful king of the Jewish nation. Like a flower blossoming on a tender stem, Jesus rises from the deeply buried, long hidden and overlooked living root of Jesse. He is of royal stock. His family tree demonstrates that to be a reality. Therefore we can address him correctly with the royal title, "Lord."*

> *We will be left as mute, as speechless as Zechariah in today's gospel when we finally come to grasp the awesome, unimaginable fact that God became flesh so that he might share his life by grafting us to himself in a life-sustaining bond: "I am the vine, you are the branches" (John 15:5). That vital, throbbing bond frees us, gives us an existence, calls us to a glory that has made us a chosen race, a royal priesthood, a people set apart from all others.*

Today we recognize our need for his abiding presence if we are to realize the purpose of our existence. And so in prayer we profoundly beg the Lord to hasten his coming to us now:

> *"Come,*
> *Flower of Jesse's stem,*
> *sign of God's love for all his people,*
> *save us without delay!"*

DECEMBER 20

Come, Key Of David

The reverent melodic strains of David's psalm praising the profound, immeasurable holiness of God provides the musical theme for the drama portrayed in the two scenes described in today's scripture proclamations. The psalm is a song of the people of the Old Testament welcoming the Ark of the Covenant, a visible sign of God's presence among his people. Our Ark of the Covenant is Mary, the boast of our humanity, who carried the presence of God within her for nine months in the process of giving God flesh in the wonder of His coming to us in the Incarnation.

> "The Lord's are the earth and its fullness;
> ... he founded it ...

> Lift up, O gates, your lintels;
>   reach up, you ancient portals,
>   that the king of glory may come in!
> Who is this king of glory?
>   The Lord of hosts; he is the king of glory."

Today's first scene is dated 734 B.C. and the narrator is Isaiah whose mission as a prophet was to proclaim the holiness of God the creator and master of all things, all persons, all nations. The menacing shadow of the mighty power of Assyria is moving ever closer towards God's people. The inhabitants of Jerusalem are in panic at the prospect that they and their kingdom will be annihilated either by the forces of the Assyrians or the combined invading armies of Aram and Israel. There seems little hope of preserving their freedom, even of saving their own lives. Their courage has left them. They have abandoned any faith in the power and promise of Yahweh to save them. They are in the depths of despair. Even the heart of Ahaz, their king, trembles at the threat of invasion and total devastation: ". . . the heart of the king and the heart of the people trembled, as the trees of the forest tremble in the wind," Isaiah comments as he approaches the king calling on him for continued trust in God's protective care. "Be calm, don't fear," the prophet urges. "Ask for a sign from the Lord, your God." But the king answers with false piety: "I will not ask! I will not tempt the Lord!" His response is that of a pious fraud, a king who had abandoned the last trace of integrity in trusting that God's age-long care of his people would continue. The king, a royal descendant of David, convinced that all was lost, that the Davidic dynasty would come to an end with his imminent destruction, rejected the offer of a clear sign not only of God's continual presence to his people but also of his unfailing intervention on their behalf.

Isaiah boldly announces to his vacillating king, Ahaz, that the child which his young queen is about to deliver will certainly assume the throne of his father, that the dynasty of David will continue because God always has and always will continue to care for his people in their unfolding history, that he will intervene even miraculously in the face of expected military invasion and total destruction. The prophecy made to David is still valid: "Your house and your kingdom will endure forever before me; your throne shall stand firm forever" (2 Samuel 7:16). God will continue to save his people. "Therefore the Lord himself will give you this sign: The virgin shall be with child, and bear a son, and shall name him Emmanuel [because 'God is with us']."

History has revealed how groundless were the fears of King Ahaz. The child prophetically referred to by Isaiah was Hezekiah who succeeded his father, Ahaz, as king of Judah in the royal line of David. Through that line God continued his caring presence to his people. The solemnity of the promise, however, and the use of the name "Emmanuel" leads us to conclude that Isaiah's view reaches far beyond the birth of Hezekiah. It ultimately focuses on the ideal king of David's line through whose coming God would definitively be with his people. In Jesus the prophecy would be perfectly realized. In the birth of Jesus from the Virgin Mary the promise is fulfilled.

It is not pious fancy to have our attention focused on Mary at this point in our Advent preparation. Hers was a vital role in God's redemptive plan. The annunciation to Mary, the teenager, described in today's gospel, confronts us with the reality that any young disciple can be a person of faith. It cannot be said: "They are too young! Give them more time!" Mary is asked to put her whole being at the service of God, to let God enter her life completely.

Mary, God's heavenly messenger waits for your answer! We too are waiting! Our future, our very life depends on your response! Mary, don't hesitate! Answer God immediately! Speak! Conceive! Embrace us by your unconditional embrace of God's will, your personal involvement in the drama of our redemption! Open your being to the Creator! Be a mother to us by giving us Life! Give us Christ, the Life!

"I am the maidservant of the Lord. Let it be done to me as you say." The angel leaves. Mary is left alone on the stage of the world, a stage bathed in an expanding brilliance, blinding to our eyes but reaching out to sweep us into its warmth, equipping us with a new vision. The actual wonder of the Incarnation has begun. God is becoming flesh. We are more than mere observers. We are participants in its purpose.

Today's Scripture Readings:

> *Isaiah 7:10-14;   Psalm 24:1-6*
> *Luke 1:26-38*

Today's Advent Prayer:

> *Throughout his reign King David defended and protected the people of his kingdom against invading armies and accomplished the unification of the Jewish people into a single nation. He foreshadowed the king who was to come, born of his royal line, Jesus the Christ, the one to be identified as the King of Kings. The promise made to him by Nathan would be fulfilled: "Your house and your kingdom will endure forever before me; your throne shall stand firm forever." The symbol of royal authority, the key and the scepter, were put into the hands of Emmanuel, "God with us."*

The Promised One, the Christ, has come not only to unlock the gates of heaven which had been securely sealed by the malice of human rebellion against the holiness and majesty of God, but also to swing wide the doors of the treasure house of divine blessings.

Today we beg for God's mercy as if none had ever been offered to humanity. We beg now because our redemption is only taking place now — only at this point in the stage of time are we personally accepting Jesus as Savior and King. We are "prisoners of darkness" pleading for release and freedom from the shackles of ignorance, aimlessness and blindness. We beg him to open our minds and hearts, unchain our selfish wills, free us from a dungeon of thick walls built by evil hearts. Give us light! Make us free! From profound depths we plead:

> *"Come,*
> *Key of David,*
> *opening the gates of God's eternal Kingdom*
> *free the prisoners of darkness!"*

DECEMBER 21

Come, Eternal Light

Tender lyrics portraying the experience of God's love fill this Advent day. In strong imagery verses from the mystical poem, the Song of Songs, excite an unfamiliar awareness that the reality of God is to be experienced. If anyone considers God to be remote and impersonal, inhuman or insensitive, unresponsive or calculating, such notions quickly evaporate with the poetic melody of today's first scripture reading. In terms of human love we hear an unusual description of the relationship between God and each one of us. The throbbing, surging imagery of the Song is often misunderstood, a cause of anxiety and discomfort for some, because a relationship with God has never been described in such an extraordinarily vivid way. Yet, understand that anyone who lives a virtuous life can enjoy such profound contact with God. St. Bernard of Clairvaux wrote that the Blessed Virgin Mary was the only creature in whom this privileged union with God was perfectly realized.

> "My lover speaks, he says to me
> 'Arise my beloved, my beautiful one, and come!
> The winter is past. . . .' "

To understand the Song it is first necessary to love. Love is not an idea. It is an experience and an action of personal faithfulness in accepting a beloved person as he or she actually is. In loving God we accept him as he is — his perfection, holiness, ongoing creativeness, merciful compassion, tender and personal care for us individually. In loving us God accepts us as we are — weak and limited, possessing a fallen humanity, each with a personal history of rebellion and unfaithfulness, but at the same time moved with an undying desire to know God, to experience God, to possess God. Such desire springs from the inherent human dignity which we have received from God, coming from his creative hands, made to his image. That reality is the basis of love of God. That reality enables God to whisper to each of us: "Arise, my beloved, my beautiful one and come!"

Such a tender expression of God's love initially leaves us speechless with wonder. There must be a response by us to God who loves us so tenderly, so intimately, so personally. The responsorial psalm gives us the means of making that reply. Joining in the words of this song we praise God for his eternal creative plan through which he personally touches and embraces us at this moment in time. Our response concludes with a promise of profound trust, recognizing that trust is a necessary ingredient in any love relationship.

> "Our soul waits for the Lord,
>   who is our help and our shield,
> For in him our hearts rejoice;
>   in his holy name we trust."

In today's gospel we accompany Mary, the expectant virgin mother, on a visit to her cousin Elizabeth. The young teenager had just responded positively to a heavenly messenger seeking her participation in a Divine plan. She was not given all the details. Mary walked the same road of faith that we are asked to walk, trusting that God knows what he's doing. She trusted God. She believed and the Incarnation event commenced. At the time of his visit to Mary the angel revealed that Elizabeth, old and sterile, was also pregnant, a sign that God can do what he wills. Therefore Mary made the long, arduous and even dangerous journey to visit Elizabeth in order to provide any personal assistance her cousin might need, to share her own joy and wonder at what was happening in her own life, and perhaps to seek advice from this woman whose life was also so dramatically touched by the hand of God. Elizabeth praises the holiness of Mary and blesses her faith in God while the child within her own womb leaps with joy as David danced in the presence of the Ark of the Covenant. John jumping with joy in the womb of Elizabeth seems to be anticipating the witness he is to make of the child now being formed in the womb of Mary.

Elizabeth's comments to Mary emphasize for us the importance of listening closely to God's word and making our personal reply to God's revealed will to us by obeying it: "Blessed is she who trusted that the Lord's words to her would be fulfilled." Mary meets the criterion of being a disciple of Jesus. She was the first disciple, the first Christian, because she was the first human being to say "yes" to Christ.

Today's Scripture Readings:

> *Song of Songs 2:8-14;   Psalm 33:2-3, 11-12, 20-21*
> *Luke 1:39-45*

Today's Advent Prayer:

> *By the light of a single glowing star guiding them the mysterious astrologers from the east were led far from home on a difficult journey, before it brought them to the presence of Jesus. "Where is the new born king of the Jews?" they had inquired. "We observed his star at its rising and have come to pay him homage" (Matthew 2:2). The sparkle of the Christmas star manifested the Lord who in time would reveal himself as the "Light of the World." "I am the light of the world. No follower of mine shall ever walk in darkness; no, he shall possess the light of life" (John 8:12).*
>
> *Jesus the Light shines into our being at his coming, stirring us to unaccustomed alertness, moving us to become radiant*

with joy. He will reveal how precious we are to his Father. He will lead us to a surprising understanding of our own inherent value. In anticipation of the wonder of the revelations we are about to experience in the Christmas feast, we are brought to the extended contemplation of today's profound prayer:

> *"O Radiant dawn,*
> *splendor of eternal light,*
> *sun of justice:*
> *come, shine on those*
> *who dwell in darkness*
> *and the shadow of death."*

DECEMBER 22

Come, King Of All Nations

Broken-hearted in her sterility, ridiculed by contemporaries because of her inability to conceive a child for a husband who loved her deeply, puzzled at God's wrath in afflicting her with barrenness, in her misery Hannah wept and prayed at the Lord's temple at Shiloh and the priest, Eli, assured her that her request would be granted by God. Within the year her prayers were answered. She became a mother and on her return to the temple Hannah dedicated her infant son to God, consecrating Samuel to lifelong temple service, giving to God the child of her dreams and prayers, the fruit of her sterility.

The responsorial psalm is replaced in today's liturgy with Hannah's hymn of praise to God on the occasion of Samuel's dedication. She glorified the omnipotent God who controls human destiny. There is a striking resemblance in Hannah's song to the Magnificat of Mary proclaimed in today's gospel. Obviously the song of Hannah was a model for the song of Mary, sharing in common the consecration of their sons to God's service. Hannah's prayerful canticle is presented in the context of having given birth to her firstborn son, whereas Mary has just conceived her firstborn.

On the occasion of the visitation Elizabeth greeted Mary with a blessing: "Blessed are you among women and blessed is the fruit of your womb." In response Mary blesses the Lord himself: "My being proclaims the greatness of the Lord. . . ." From the profound depths of the teenage virgin's spirit a song of praise surges in response to God's holiness, power and creativeness. Permitting God to intervene in her life, with a fullness of trust, Mary has put her total being at God's disposal, her intact virginity involved in the extra-ordinary process of being transformed into fruitfulness. She acknowledges the creative, mighty arm of God which has touched her personally as he touches each of his creatures in the unfolding wonder of their existence.

As her prayer begins Mary describes herself once again as the servant of the Lord, precisely as she responded to the angel Gabriel at her annunciation. We should be aware that "servant" or "handmaiden" are significant terms. Mary uses the feminine form of "slave" to describe herself, thereby identifying herself with the earliest Christians, the disciples of the Lord who were "nothings" in the world — unwanted, having neither social nor legal status, lowly creatures of the times. Such a mentality dominates this prayer of Mary:

> "He has shown might with his arm;
>> he has confused the proud . . .
> He has deposed the mighty . . .
>> and raised the lowly to high places.
> The hungry he has given every good . . .
>> while the rich he has sent empty away."

The Magnificat anticipates the gospel message of Jesus in the beatitudes:

"Blest are you poor; the reign of God is yours.
Blest are you who hunger; you shall be filled.
Blest are you who are weeping; you shall laugh.
Blest are you when men hate you . . . your reward shall be
    great in heaven.

Woe to you rich; for your consolation is now.
Woe to you who are full; you shall go hungry.
Woe to you who laugh now; you shall weep in your grief.
Woe to you when all speak well of you. Their fathers
    treated the false prophets in just this way."
    (Luke 6:20-26)

In her canticle Mary makes a statement about discipleship and about the gospel. Mary, the first disciple of Jesus, tells us that as disciples we are to demonstrate discipleship to others, beginning from the point of what it means to be a "servant" of God.

The prayer springing from Mary's spirit should be ours also. To the extent we possess her spirit of reverence and trust, Mary's song will be ours as well.

> "My being proclaims the greatness of the Lord,
> My spirit finds joy in God my savior . . .
> God who is mighty has done great things for me,
> holy is his name."

Today's Scripture Readings:

1 Samuel 1:24-28;   1 Samuel 2:1, 4-8
Luke 1:46-56

Today's Advent Prayer:

It's a fact of life that every single person has been lifted into existence by the creative hand of God. The reality cannot be denied that our origin is from the dust of the earth. That's a human fact. And so is the reality that the tragedy of sinful unfaithfulness and rebellion has necessitated the need for atonement and redemption in order to achieve acceptable reconciliation with our offended Divine Creator. Therefore we pray today: "Save the creature you fashioned from the dust."

Sin offends the holiness and goodness of God and drives a wedge into the unity of the human family. The reality that we are one family is little understood and usually overlooked. Generally our sense of God's kingdom has an individual and selfish view. We need the King to come to unite us not only to his Father but also to each other. As we approach the celebration of the Lord's historical Nativity, his coming to each one of us now at this moment of our lives, and most particularly as we look forward to his coming at the end of time, may the King find us eagerly watching and waiting, ready to welcome him with full acceptance. Today all nations, all peoples, call out to share in the promised kingdom.

"O, King of all nations,
source of your Church's unity and faith:
Come,
save all mankind,
your own creation!"

DECEMBER 23

Come, Emmanuel

A man of striking appearance strides to the center of the Advent stage. His voice is strong, his words direct and blunt, easily understood by anyone who gives him their attention. His name is Malachi. He is called "The Messenger" and he speaks for Yahweh. The year is 460 B.C. The prophet Malachi challenges the religious indifference, the scandalous abuses and injustices committed against God and their fellow Israelites by those who describe themselves as the "People of God," especially those who should know better — the educated, the political and religious leaders, people of privilege and comfort.

"The Messenger" reminds his audience of God's historical intervention in the life of his people. As God spoke to them in the past he will speak once again. As God led them once he will lead them again. As he bound himself in sacred covenant with them in their past history he will make a new binding covenant with them once again. Malachi promises that acceptable worship will one day be offered with the Lord gloriously present in their company.

As "The Messenger" concludes his script and steps back
into the shadows of history we hear an echo of Jesus' voice
identifying John the Baptist as "My Messenger" (Luke
7:37). In time we will learn as Malachi had foretold that the
sacrifices at the temple in Jerusalem and the Levitical
priestly office exercised there will be transformed and
perfected, surpassed and completed by the very presence of
God. Jesus, God who became flesh, is the fulfillment of
Malachi's prophecy. He alone as priest and victim will make
a perfectly acceptable sacrificial offering to atone for the
malice of rebellion against the majesty of God. The world
waits for his coming.

The audience, and we're part of it, now momentarily
waits in silence. However, it's only for a very brief space of
time until the softly sung petition of the psalmist grows
stronger with a growing multitude of voices pleading for the
promised Savior to come to us and give the desperately
needed guidance which only he can provide: "Your ways, O
Lord, make known to me . . . Guide me . . . teach me."

The revelation of Divine power, the wonder and extent
of his mercy in the coming of the Promised One has a
prelude in the birth of John the Baptist, the messenger of
the New Covenant, recounted for us in today's gospel.
"What will this child be?" they ask. In time John will fulfill
his mission of preparing the people of the world for Jesus:
"Make ready the way of the Lord." "Reform your lives! The
reign of God is at hand." It will also be John's mission as
"The Messenger" to introduce Jesus to the world: "Behold
the Lamb of God." In conferring the title, "Lamb," John was
unconsciously revealing Jesus' future fulfillment of
Malachi's promise of an acceptable worship which would be
offered one day when the Lord would be gloriously present
in the company of humanity. Today's Advent scenario
leaves us breathless with wonder and anticipation.

> "Lift up your heads and see:
> your redemption is near at hand."
> (Response to today's Psalm)

Today's Scripture Readings:

*Malachi 3:1-4, 23-24; Psalm 25:4-5, 8-10, 14
Luke 1:57-66*

Today's Advent Prayer:

A prayer is wrenched from the depths of hungering spirits, rushing to the lips of an anxious, expectant humanity: "Come, Emmanuel. . . ."

The last of the special Advent petitions, the "O Antiphons," which have been our special prayer focus for the past eight days, unites us today with the rest of humanity in profound adoration of our God. "Come, Emmanuel, God's presence among us. . . ."

In the brightness and wonder of God's presence we are overwhelmed with a vivid awareness that rebellious conduct against the holiness, majesty, goodness, perfection and clearly revealed will of our God and Creator screams out for reparation. Appropriate atonement can only be accomplished by someone who not only is akin to the Divine Person offended but the one who at the same time is akin to, on the level of, the offender. The redeemer who is able to repair the fracture of human sin must live, have existence, in the world of God as well as in the world of humanity. Is that a wild notion? An impossible dream? A vague hope? A vain aspiration? We pray: "Come, Emmanuel, God's presence among us . . . save us, Lord our God."

The Lord's coming is imminent. Tomorrow is Christmas eve and on the following day with joyous wonder and gratitude we will participate in a celebration of the Lord's birth at Bethlehem 2000 years ago. The day by day preparation for the Christmas celebration during these weeks of Advent has led as well to an awareness of the reality of the Lord's coming to each of us in a special, personal way at this moment in our existence. Jesus is coming to us now personally and individually in a way that he has never come to us before. In addition, looking to the future we anticipate his final coming in glory at the end of time as our judge. "Come, Emmanuel, God's presence among us, our King, our Judge." We pledge our loyalty to our king and our obedience to him who will be our judge. Our prayer today will eventually conclude in an "Amen" which will echo throughout eternity in the halls of God's kingdom.

"Come . . . save us." As the world once anxiously waited for the Promised One to come, from the depths of our spirits a yearning cry now rises: "Come . . . save us."

He and we draw closer, nearer to each other. The Lord will soon be with us in a way we never shared his presence in the past. From the searching, hungering depths of our spirits a prayer reaches our lips:

> *"O Emmanuel*
> *God's presence among us,*
> *our King, our Judge:*
> *Come, save us, Lord our God!"*

DECEMBER 24

Come, Bread Of Life

Under David's leadership the kingdoms of Judah and Israel had been successfully united. Invading armies had been destroyed and the borders of the land were made secure against enemy attacks. King David had taken up residence in his palace in the capital city of Jerusalem which he established as the religious center of the nation and a source of unity for the people with the dramatic transfer there of the Ark of the Covenant, the visual symbol of God's presence to his people. Yet, David couldn't rest contented, troubled by the need of providing a more suitable edifice for God's presence in the midst of his people. Therefore he proposed building a temple which would more fittingly correspond to the majesty and glory of God. That proposal was rejected by God with the explanation that he was dependent on David for nothing whereas David was dependent on him for everything. Nathan the prophet relayed that decision to David coupled with a Divine reassurance that his royal dynasty would last forever. A question regarding a "house of God" received an answer relative to the "house of David."

> "The Lord also reveals to you that he will establish a house for you. Your house and your kingdom shall endure forever before me; your throne shall stand firm forever."

David's dream of a suitable "house of God" became a reality with the construction of the magnificent temple at Jerusalem during the reign of his successor son, King Solomon.

The extraordinary promise about his dynasty delivered by God to the "house of David" by the prophet Nathan found its fulfillment as the muted lips of Zechariah began to speak in praise of God when he conferred a name on his newly born son, John. That name was given as directed by the angel Gabriel at the annunciation to Zechariah which took place in the "house of God," the Holy Place, in Solomon's temple at Jerusalem.

Zechariah's prophecy, directed to the "God of Israel," describes the work of the Messiah in Old Testament terms. The promises made to Abraham and David are recalled. The redemption achieved by the king who was born of David's royal family is praised. This prayer of praise clearly demonstrates that salvation is a fulfillment of the promises made to Abraham and David. Zechariah leaves no doubt that salvation was not brought about by his son, John, but by the person for whom his son prepares the way.

Listening to Zechariah's announcement we are left with a probing question: Are these the actual words of Zechariah or are we reciting a prayer which perhaps our ancient ancestors in the faith, the earliest Jewish converts to Christianity used when they gathered together as the infant Church to praise God? Are Zechariah's words of praise to the God of Israel actually the words of praise of the very first Christians? Is this canticle which we have come to know as the Benedictus a hymn of the early Jewish Christians which Luke has put on the lips of Zechariah in his gospel account of the Good News?

That is merely a speculation, an educated guess, based on the content of Zechariah's canticle. Its content seems to lead to such a conclusion. Whatever the fact, the Benedictus today seems to be a most appropriate gospel proclamation to bring our Advent experience to its termination. Upon

reflection it would even seem to be a synopsis of that profound experience.

> "Blessed be the Lord the God of Israel
>> because he has visited and ransomed his people.
> He has raised a horn of saving strength for us
>> in the house of David his servant . . .
> And you, O child, shall be called
>> prophet of the Most High;
> For you shall go before the Lord
>> to prepare straight paths for him. . . ."

Today's Scripture Readings:

*2 Samuel 7:1-5, 8-11, 16;   Psalm 89:2-5, 27, 29
Luke 1:67-79*

Today's Advent Prayer:

*Jesus was born of the house of David: "And so Joseph went
from the town of Nazareth in Galilee to Judea, to David's
town of Bethlehem — because he was of the house and
lineage of David — to register with Mary, his espoused wife,
who was with child. While they were there the days of her
confinement were completed. She gave birth to her first-born
son." (Luke 2:4-7)*

*That was a night of divine surprises when a virgin had a
baby, when shepherds had visions, when an army of angels
flew with song through the night sky over Bethlehem and
when age-old promises were fulfilled.*

*Of the "house of David," Jesus was born in David's city,
Bethlehem. The literal translation of the name of the city,
Bethlehem, is "house of bread." King David's proposal for a*

*fitting "house of God," therefore, ultimately would be ful-
filled by the one born in the "house of bread." Jesus would in
time explain:*

> *"I myself am the living bread . . .
> If anyone eats this bread he shall live forever . . .
> The bread I will give you is my flesh . . .
> The man who feeds on my flesh . . . remains in
>   me and I in him . . .
> This is the bread that came down from heaven."*
>
> *(John 6:25-59)*

*The place where God wants to dwell is in the fabric of the
lives of his people. He wants to be there in that house. It is
there, in those personal, individual and profound depths,
that he would reign as king. That is the final Divine surprise
which comes from Bethlehem. God came in his way in the
wonder of God becoming flesh. God comes to us still, "the
bread that has come down from heaven."*

*The stage is now set for the appearance of Jesus. His pre-
cursor, John the Baptist, is announced, makes his appearance. The drama of redemption is about to commence.
Peace, joy and hope are in the air. They are the atmosphere
of the Christmas coming which is about to happen. Our
waiting is about to end. The gift of Christmas will soon be
ours. Come, Jesus! Welcome!*

> *"This is what we proclaim to you:*
>> *what was from the beginning,*
>> *what we have heard,*
>> *what we have seen with our eyes,*
>> *what we have looked upon*
>> *and our hands have touched —*
>>> *we speak of the word of life.*

> *"This life became visible;*
>> *we have seen and bear witness to it,*
>> *and we proclaim to you the eternal life*
>> *that was present to the Father*
>> *and became visible to us."*
>>>> *(1 John 1:1-2)*

An Interesting Thought

The publication you have just finished reading is part of the apostolic efforts of the Society of St. Paul of the American Province. The Society of St. Paul is an international religious community located in 23 countries, whose particular call and ministry is to bring the message of Christ to all people through the communications media.

Following in the footsteps of their patron, St. Paul the Apostle, priests and brothers blend a life of prayer and technology as writers, editors, marketing directors, graphic designers, bookstore managers, pressmen, sound engineers, etc. in the various fields of the mass media, to announce the message of Jesus.

If you know a young man who might be interested in a religious vocation as a brother or priest and who shows talent and skill in the communications arts, ask him to consider our life and ministry. For more information at no cost or obligation write:

Vocation Office
2187 Victory Blvd.
Staten Island, NY 10314-6603
Telephone: (718) 698-3698